SAY

WHAT

YOU

LOVE

Unconditionally

See
only
peace

Hear only peace

Speak
only
peace

SAY WHAT YOU LOVE

Unconditionally

A Guide to Creating
Anything You Love

Mackenzie Jordan

Diamond Heart Books
Scottsdale, AZ

This edition published by:
Diamond Heart Books
9393 North 90th Street, Suite 102-158, Scottsdale, Arizona 85258
web sites: SayWhatYouLove.com ❤ YourPeaceCounts.com

Say What You Love and Your Peace Counts
are trademarks of Mackenzie Jordan.

Cover Design: Jeffrey Couglar
Creator Comic Artist: Julia Kirkby

All attempts were made to credit authors of quotes accurately. Any corrections are appreciated and may be submitted to the publisher. Thank you.

Say What You Love (SWYL) is not a license for, and does not grant permission for, disrespecting others or their property. Imposing one's self on others in any way, or hurting yourself or others, is not implied or supported by the SWYL concept. Any such misinterpretation is a mistake and is the responsibility of the user to correct. Applying Say What You Love responsibly requires your common sense, intelligence, and sense of respect.

Printed in Canada

ISBN 0-9661044-2-0

FIRST EDITION

For peace within —
and globally

Acknowledgments

I love to appreciate my cheerleaders Marcella Hughes and Elizabeth Rosenburg for their phenomenal support and loving care of me and SAY WHAT YOU LOVE. Their excitement and dedication held me in a womb of love from the gestation through the creation of SAY WHAT YOU LOVE (SWYL).

I whole-heartedly thank Cynthia Turner who I feel is my own personal angel of love and light. Thanks to Wade Starr for his amazing commitment to humanitarian projects like SWYL. And much gratitude to Shayla Roberts who is an abundant source of loving reflection and inspiration. Thank you to Roger Ripps who is always there in friendship and in keeping my laptop tiptop. Thanks to J'lein Liese for her bright light and generosity of spirit during the marinating phase of SWYL.

Say What You Love was written during the fall of 2002 on the volcanic Big Island of Hawaii, where the lava flows forth with new creation, the Aloha spirit is alive with juiciness, and raw, rural surroundings encourage simpler living. Thanks to the Kalani Honua Community and all the staff and work-scholars living there who made my writing time so healing and stimulating. I especially wish to acknowledge Qallah for her solar radiance, Sylvie for her precious presence, Ann and Babette for proof-reading, Carrie for the many ways she welcomed me so graciously, and Peggy for wheels. With extra aloha to Elizabeth Corrigan for her charismatic enthusiasm and wonderful gifts of editing insight, and to Ron Carter for his many kindnesses. And to Jenoa— a dear bright light.

To my miracle workers: Marilee Crocker, thanks for her insightful editing, humor in the trenches, and especially for her wise kindness; Julia Kirkby for her wonderful expressive drawings; Jeffrey Couglar for his passionate cover design infused with the island's big love; and to Anthony Cianciolo for being my creative hero with all his eleventh-hour magic.

Thanks to Jason Purcell for joyfully sharing his inspiring and memorable mottoes. (I caught one.) I also wish to thank Larry and Candy Tree for their early support and encouragement of SAY WHAT YOU LOVE. Much gratitude to Francis Shovel Shinn, a woman ahead of her time who left a beautiful legacy for future generations to discover.

I am grateful to Byron Katie for the playground she created

for *loving what is* through her process — The Work. And I love to appreciate the tremendous gift that SAY WHAT YOU LOVE is for me; for in knowing and saying what I love, I connect with a simple clear peace.

Thank you to all my friends and clients who tried out the SAY WHAT YOU LOVE principles and shared them with others. This book is rooted in their enthusiasm and gracious reports of transformation, breakthroughs and miracles.

I send out my gratitude in advance to all of you who share, teach or bring SAY WHAT YOU LOVE into communities all around the world. You are the roots and wings of peace on our planet. And before we are done awakening the deep wells of love within and around us, there will be millions contributing *their* peace to our world's peace. *I lovvve that!*

And to the divine energy that is awakening in all of us.

To all of you, mahalo nui loa, aloha

~Mackenzie Jordan
March 6, 2003, Hawaii

Contents

In the beginning   1
Basic Ingredients   9
The Vision   20

CHAPTER 1   25
What is SWYL?
Why should I say what I love?
Gold or garbage
What is this thing called love?
Tell the truth faster; have a good life
Pay now
Room for Miracles
A radical perspective

CHAPTER 2   49
SWYL In Action
The effort to *not* get what you want
Beyond complaining
How do you know you love something?
What If I don't know what I love?
Tag. You're it!
Breathe love
SWYLisms

CHAPTER 3   71
Don't Believe Everything You Think
Change the channel
It's only a parade
Listening to anxiety or peace
When it hurts— inquire
Justifying, proving, etc.
Feeling worthy is not required to SWYL
Better than immunity

CHAPTER 4   90
Creator Comics
The downward spiral of anti-creating
Ok God, here's my wish list
. . .as if *that* will help
God hears you
Worrying about jerks
You get to choose
Power manifesting
When affirmations don't work
That's too easy!

Chapter 5   123

As You Wish

Simon says
The power of prayer
Your word is your wand
Go straight to what you love!

Chapter 6   133

Solve Problems or Create Miracles

Train your mind
Two wolves
The allure of solving problems
If you have enough time to worry . . .
To create or not create
Clues that you are anti-creating
Creation mode ~ a simpler plan

Chapter 7   149

The Power of Love

Practices for mastery
"I wonder what I love now?"
Be a reporter of What You Love
Report what you love
Pretend no one can hear you
Making room for love
Many kinds of clutter
Ask others what they love
How would your life be different
The Power of Meditation
The Power of loving Self
I hear what you don't want

**The Glossary of Creation
and Anti Creation Words**   169

If we ourselves remain angry and then sing world peace, it has little meaning. First, our individual self must learn peace. This we can practice. Then, we can teach the rest of the world.

~The Dalai Lama

In the beginning

Say What You Love (SWYL) was born out of a lifelong shopping assignment to find myself some peace of mind. I never enjoyed worrying and controlling things to try to feel safe—it hurt—but I unconsciously did it anyway. It seemed so darned automatic.

In mid summer 2000, the idea that started out as *Tell Me What You Love!* woke me from a dream and insisted on voicing itself. It clearly had a visionary life of its own. That summer, a dozen dazzling projects and writing assignments sprang to mind out of the blue—all of which I dutifully wrote down in outline form under "future projects." But two weeks after the Tell Me What You Love! idea came, this one was not content to stay put in the to-do file. It wanted to be written. Right now! So in August, I cleared two weeks to begin writing and went to a little town in New Mexico called Truth or Consequences, which sits on the hot springs land of the Rio Grande.

When I got home to Phoenix the whole thing went dormant, including the urgency—until the winter holidays. During a New Year's retreat, it occurred to me that Tell Me What You

Love!, which by then had evolved to Say What You Love, had other ideas for itself. It wanted to be a simpler, humorous little book. *Okay*.

And still it would be another year and a half before much more movement happened on it. Apparently, I had to attend SWYL boot camp first! This meant the book was going nowhere until I spent more quality time saying what I loved instead of what I didn't love. *Okay*.

Throughout the writing process, all flow ceased whenever I ventured the least bit off track from the simple message of Say What You Love. I'm telling you, SWYL was strict. It knew what it wanted. I learned a lot about listening during this process, and about what happens when you don't listen.

Before the dream defined SWYL as a writing project, it began as a signature question I often put to complaining clients: "Okay, I hear what you don't want. Now, tell me what you love!" At this point, it was revealing itself as the personal assignment I was seeking for myself.

I had to write Say What You Love for me, because I needed it. Even while writing SWYL, and during the whole boot camp period and beyond, I discover countless places where the language I unconsciously use betrays what I love and care about. No wonder getting what I wanted was so hit and miss.

Luckily, perfection need not be the goal for me or for you. Simply noticing one's limiting language and self talk, then shifting to what you love, one statement at a time, creates amazing magic. It's enough to focus increasing amounts of attention on acknowledging and saying what you love. When you forget to say what you love, you can gently remind yourself.

A juicy, fool-proof language for creating anything you love

To put your attention on what you want—instead of what you do not want—is not exactly a fresh idea. To realize that your language binds you to its fate is not a new concept. To put e-motion or passion behind your intention or prayer—again, not new. Yet Say What You Love streamlines all the best of those ingredients into a juicy, fool-proof language of self-expression, love, and inner peace.

I cherish anyone who takes Say What You Love to heart. I know you will receive more blessings and abundance than you dreamed possible. What could be more precious, priceless and freeing than to know and say what you love and then live it?

Saying What You Love will alter the way you experience life and, in some cases, alter the course of your life. Birth, death and other changes will still happen—this impermanence of life is one of our great teachers—but through it all, Saying What You Love will enlighten your perception of those events. There is something to love in any situation you find yourself in. The choice is yours—to worry, to complain, or to love.

Go Gently

I invite you to be gentle with yourself, especially if acknowledging what you love is new territory for you.

And please be patient with those who have difficulty listening to you Say What You Love. It may be even harder for them to hear you Say What You Love than it was for you to start saying it. Change is scary sometimes.

Imagine a scenario like this:

John and Maria have been nagging one another throughout 38 years of marriage. It's so familiar to them that they've become comfortable with it. When Maria begins Saying What She Loves, in many ways their intimacy improves immediately. But John fears that his safe life is changing, and he doesn't know how to play his part anymore. He starts to fear that he will be left behind.

The one true conspiracy:
glorious beauty
everywhere to enjoy
and breathe by,
hidden
in plain sight
from those who
would prefer a picture.

While Maria is discovering the many things she loves more than nagging, she can be kind to John, even if John keeps nagging and has not yet decided to Say What He Loves. If they can allow for their differences, they can enjoy staying together. Everyone chooses what works best for them. That's okay.

During these times of threats, war and terrorists—when people are very scared—be gentle. It's scary to feel scared. When they are out of touch with what they love, scared people can react chaotically from their fear and anger.

Imagine another scenario: When Michael begins Saying What He Loves—let's say on a coffee break when everyone is talking about war—his work mates may at first believe he isn't taking the subject seriously. In reality, Michael may be the only one in that conversation who understands the principle of: You get what you pay attention to.

Be gentle with yourself, especially if anyone accuses you or confuses you with someone they inwardly fear themselves to be.

Not everyone will understand the power of Say What You Love. *That's okay.* To them SWYL will seem lightweight or even worthless, and for them, for now, it is. So don't worry about the naysayers or about changing their minds. Simply Say What You

Love for your own enjoyment. That's plenty. And it is enough to transform your world.

Instead of placing your attention on worry or fear about dramatic happenings, focus on what you feel drawn to do to help. Other than that, no need to worry. Worry does not help! Well that's not *exactly* true. You do help when you worry: You help to bring into being whatever you worry about.

Put your attention on what you love — no matter what you are hearing in the news. Use Say What You Love to navigate especially in times of confusion or chaos. Show us a new way to be and think. Inspire peace by Saying What You Love.

"Anxiety is praying for what you don't want."

~Old Hawaiian Saying

This is an amazing time in history!

We can be fearful, like it's the end of the world, or we can be very excited about ending our own limited thinking and begin to act like the creator beings we are. Truly, there has never been a better time for shifting the switch from *fear* to *love*.

The *power of love* has barely been tapped as a source of transformative energy. It's been mostly bottled up!

Hey!

You know how to uncork a bottle, don't you?

The Words That Create Us

In living Say What You Love, a deeper respect and fascination with words is growing in me. The words we choose have meaning and power. They affect our perceptions and whether we feel abundant or blocked, free or limited. A Glossary in the back of this book defines common words we throw around quite casually everyday, often without realizing how our choice of words either empowers or limits the very dreams we try so hard to achieve.

I invite you to become familiar with the Glossary before you begin reading Say What You Love and to take advantage of the Glossary while reading. The words you use are your bond by promising your energy. They commit you accordingly—and they work for you exactly like currency. Can you afford language that results in extra work for you, puts you behind schedule, or makes you feel badly about yourself?

What will you be purchasing with your language today?

Feel free to consult a dictionary for other words you use not found in the Glossary. Discover for yourself if your words limit you or create for you What You Love.

And by the way, you can pronounce SWYL as *swell*.

*She was so bankrupt,
she couldn't even afford
a negative thought.*

~Sheryl Jai

Basic Ingredients

SAY WHAT YOU LOVE (SWYL)

has three basic ingredients:

· · · · · · · · · · · · · · ·

Knowing
what
you
love

Saying
what
you
love

Living
what
you
love

Acknowledging what you love unconditionally, without needing to justify it, is a core piece of SAY WHAT YOU LOVE (SWYL).

Giving voice to what you love, whether vocally or silently, is another part of SWYL.

The gift of gifts is *to allow yourself* to feel that much love, to live what you love.

Giving yourself What You Love happens the very moment you give up thinking about what you need or must have in order to be happy, and instead choose to notice what you love. Do you think that sounds too simple to make a difference in your life? Well, sometimes it's the simplest shifts in perspective that can effect the most profound change.

Though each of these steps may, at first, be easier said than done, with practice Saying What You Love starts feeling more natural than not saying what you love.

In the meantime, this entire book is devoted to helping you get in touch with what you love, even if you think you have forgotten or outgrown love.

So, what does it mean to "get in touch" with what you love? What is Love?

Love is your native intelligence

To live What You Love is to return to a state of original innocence — that place we all experienced before we learned to distrust our native intelligence, defer to others, and worry. Worry is common, but it's not natural. Love is natural. If you're concerned that living what you love will foster irresponsibility or laziness, rest assured: To love honestly is to bring responsibility to every part of your life. When you live What You Love, you gain a profound sense of authentic responsibility to yourself, a responsibility that supports the spiritual purpose of your life and honors the integrity of your well-being.

Living What You Love brings a wondrous joy and inspiration to your loved ones, though at first glance you may fear you'll appear selfish or foolish. However, the power of love is palpable. Soon, you'll experience how uplifting and life-transforming it is, even when you just spend time with someone who is living What They Love. It's contagious!

When you Say What You Love
you access pure creation

Saying What You Love provides the fuel for creating anything you love unconditionally.

The creative power of SWYL cannot be used to cause harm. The very idea to cause harm, chaos or fear is contrary to love and to SWYL.

Saying What You Love is an act of love with no other motive but love itself.

We are shaped and
fashioned by what we love.

~Johann Wolfgang von Goethe

Say What You Love as:

A concept to live by: Say What You Love (SWYL) is your acknowledgment of what you love—unconditionally—without justification, reservation, or argument. Saying What You Love is inner peace. SWYL is simply a profound way of living as a positive, creative force of power. When you connect to What You Love, it is present in how you talk, perceive, behave and envision. Saying What You Love empowers your well-being, relationships, and life purpose, as well as your experience of joy and success.

A manifesting tool: Saying What You Love bypasses the limitations, expectations and negative habits that sneakily limit your brilliance, visionary abilities, joy, financial abundance and success. When you Say What You Love, you give voice to your deepest truths. In this way you access the most powerful creative force there is. SWYL has unlimited potential for actualizing miracles in your life.

A vision for global peace: Say What You Love (SWYL) is an experiment in shifting our entire collective consciousness from a predominantly negative and victim-focused mentality to a creator being way of interacting with one another. By Saying What You Love when addressing current affairs—whether in your own home or when making decisions in your neighborhood, drafting international treaties, or ensuring clean water, food, fair commerce and actualized sovereignty for all beings—you align your focus and energy with the most potent energy in the universe. In doing so, you create conditions for global peace.

Creator Being: *n.*

One who acknowledges, accepts and actualizes their role as a creator.

One who employs their native intelligence and ability to envision creations into existence.

One who perceives, envisions, or behaves with creative power and intent.

Other ways to apply SWYL:

As a model for well-being: Saying What You Love allows you to exist harmoniously within your heart, mind, body, emotions and beingness and to live authentically. When you Say What You Love, you align with your unlimited natural resources of health, insight and vitality. Your intuitive accuracy and sense of inner peace naturally deepen because you are acknowledging, not denying, what you know and love.

As a model for clear communication: When you Say What You Love, you honor anyone you speak to. When you listen to someone who shares with you what he or she loves unconditionally, you create an opportunity for uncommon closeness and miraculous healing. When each party clearly acknowledges What They Love unconditionally, and without justification, then making plans, agreements, vows or contracts requires no manipulation, pressure or painful compromise on either side. You automatically bypass many situations that are not in your best interest.

As a practice for mindfulness: Saying What You Love invites you to pay attention to What You Love unconditionally.

This is especially helpful during times when your *machine mind* (automatic negative thinking) is persuading you to believe its convincing barrage of worries. When you Say What You Love, you become fully grounded in the present moment, rather than losing yourself in worries or fantasies about the past or future.

As a spiritual practice: Saying What You Love is a path toward unconditional acceptance and kindness. Knowing the truth about What You Love frees you from the illusion that you should fulfill other people's expectations. Discovering that you love to know what other people love unconditionally also can release you from a lifelong habit of imposing your expectations on, and thereby rudely manipulating, the very people you say you love most. Thus SWYL is a path of freedom and kindness.

As a healing modality: Saying What You Love relieves you of the energetic debt created when you compromise your physical or psychological health by arguing for your worries, limitations and problems. The harmony created by Saying What You Love has a calming, healing effect on the body.

As a basis for making choices: In matters large and small—from where to go to eat or how to decorate your home to questions of career, marriage and family—Saying What You Love cuts through mental confusion, indecision and the fear of making a mistake. Imagine, never justifying yourself again! *What would you do with all that extra energy?*

Hear only peace

See only peace

Speak only peace

THE VISION

of

SAY WHAT YOU LOVE *Unconditionally*

Global peace.

Beginning from within,

one being at a time.

Be cause . . . YOUR PEACE COUNTS.

Be the *cause* of peace happening!

What if a certain number of people—unified by their belief in the power of love—could change the course of the future?

Perhaps it's not so difficult to imagine if we consider a small boat built for six passengers. What if all six passengers sat on one side of the boat? Would it tip over? Probably not, because the boat was designed to safely carry six. But if we keep adding weight to that same side, there will come a point when just one more person will tip it over, right? The tipping point may be the tenth person or the twentieth, but we know it will tip at some point. At that point, critical mass has been reached. *Critical mass* is a scientific term, defined in Webster's as an amount necessary or sufficient to have a significant effect or to achieve a result or produce a chain reaction.

The Hundredth Monkey, a fable based on a scientific study, tells a remarkable story that illustrates the power and potential of critical mass. It tells of Japanese monkeys who lived on separate islands and had no direct contact with one another. The monkeys shared similar eating habits until, on one of the islands, one monkey began washing her sweet potatoes before eating them. Soon her mother, and then other monkeys on the island, began mimicking her and washing their potatoes too. One day, when a critical mass of 100 monkeys on that island were wash-

SAY WHAT YOU LOVE *Unconditionally*

ing their potatoes, suddenly all the monkeys on that island began washing their potatoes. The real surprise came when monkeys on all the other islands spontaneously began washing their potatoes too.

Remember, they lived across the water and never saw the original monkeys washing potatoes. So how did those monkeys gain that knowledge? It may sound like magic, but it actually points to how connected we all are. And it demonstrates that when a critical number of people gains an awareness, that awareness spreads to everyone.

Someone did the math for what the critical mass point would be for all humanity. How many human beings would need to learn a new skill before we reached critical mass—the point where each member of humanity spontaneously adopts that new skill, without consciously learning it or seeing it done by anyone else? The number is one million people.

The theory is that when one million people learn a particular skill or embrace a new thought form, that ability (or wisdom) becomes effortlessly available to the rest of the population.

So here's the auspicious vision:

As one million people begin to acknowledge and Say What They Love unconditionally, all around the globe, on all the islands and continents—*every* human will begin spontaneously and effortlessly to live what they love also.

And the world is forever changed.

In this way, Say What You Love is a grand experiment in both global and inner peace.

SAY WHAT YOU LOVE

Unconditionally

~ a way of being whose time has come ~

And, if the **what if** experiment doesn't appeal to you, you're still invited to enjoy the SWYL feel-good benefits.

Chapter One

What Is

Say What You Love?

There is no greater invitation
to love than loving first.

~St. Augustine

Why should I say what I love?

There wouldn't be a need to take a natural way-of-being such as live What You Love and turn it into a concept like SWYL, except for the quirky little fact that we usually say the opposite.

That's where it all breaks down, right there, isn't it? We become accustomed to automatically judging, negating and compromising, as if that's the way to accomplish things or to get along. We dwell on what we "should" want or need, as if that will help us feel accepted or respected. We do these things instead of trusting that what we love is good enough to succeed, good enough to be accepted.

One hears: "What's wrong with you? You're supposed to want a good life for yourself, get a career that will make you lots of money." A point of view like that is fine if it is what you love, but it presumes that you want to make a lot of money, which may not be your truth. Some people love things other than chasing money or collecting material toys. They love simple living. And that's okay.

By Saying What You Love, you bypass a considerable amount of hassle surrounding getting your authentic needs met. Navigating life simply seems a lot easier when you Say What You Love.

I've learned . . .
that no one is perfect until
you fall in love with them.

~Andy Rooney

SWYL is distinct from the use of affirmations, positive thinking and goal-setting. If these tactics were not successful for you in the past, don't be surprised. Used properly they can be helpful. But no doubt a particular ingredient was missing in those failed situations—one that is vital to any vision or goal coming into being. The ingredient is knowing what you love and Saying What You Love, either silently or aloud.

SWYL is also different from saying what you *want* or *need*. Words like *want* and *need* send out a vibration of poverty—and that's what you get in return. (Remember to consult the glossary for your everyday words.)

And though What You Love can be the same as what you prefer, it's not necessarily the case. That's because sometimes your preferences originate in worries about what you "should" want, perhaps in hopes of being liked or appreciated. But these preferences do not express your authentic self, and because they lack the honesty and clarity of What You Love, they are less powerful. When you Say What You Love, you send out a clear, strong signal, creating a higher-voltage energy charge.

The fewer our wants, the more we resemble the Gods.

~Socrates

Try this to gauge
whether or not you have found
What You Love:

Is someone challenging what you say you prefer, want or need? Is that making you begin to doubt yourself? Then you are not expressing What You Love yet.

Where there is love, no argument can talk you out of it. You love; that's it. You need no reason why you love something.

However, if you feel you do need a reason, or feel you must defend why, no problem. Just go a little deeper until you connect with what you really love unconditionally.

The heart has reasons
that reason does not
understand

~Jacques Benigue Bonssuet

Saying What You Love sends out

a high-voltage energy charge

that is infinitely more powerful

than saying what you

need, want or desire

Gold or garbage

When you are trying to get your needs met and you say you *need* or *want* something, you are claiming that you don't have that thing. *Duh. Right!* Yet, the words you choose to express yourself are either like gold or garbage when it comes to getting what you want. Let's take a look.

Have you ever heard of the universal law that says, "You get what you pay attention to?" It goes something like this: When you say, "I *need* more money," instead of getting the money, you get the experience of *needing* more money. *(Thanks a lot!)* However, *needing* is exactly what you asked for.

Love is God's vibration. When you Say What You Love you are speaking God's language. It's not that Saying What You Love makes it easier for God to fulfill your order; *God can do anything, right?* But, when you Say What You Love, you make it *possible* for God to fulfill your order, as if you are giving your blessing.

I just need enough to tide me over until I need more.

~ Bill Hoest

When your prayers and requests are not answered to your satisfaction, it's not because God is denying you. It's a signal that you are still focused on *wanting* and *needing*, on being deprived, rather than on loving. It's a mistake to feel personally rejected or abandoned by God.

Your *free will* ties God's hands from "making up" or "filling in" the missing pieces of what you were *really* trying to say or request.

Creation (God) delivers *exactly* what you ask for. That's the good news and the *oh-no* news! God mirrors your thinking and intention. The clearer you are, the more supportive and helpful God seems to be, which makes you more receptive to God's partnership.

Mankind's greatest gift,
also its greatest curse,
is that we have free choice.
We can make our choices
built from love or from fear.

~Elizabeth Kubler-Ross

When you Say What You Love

you open up

clear channels of communication

Here's what to do:

Your primary "job" is to walk through your day noticing and Saying What You Love. That's it!

You start wherever you are. Practice SWYL in the good and happier times for easier use during the challenging times. Make Saying What You Love such a part of your experience that it becomes as automatic as worrying *used* to be.

How or when What You Love will manifest is not your concern. Along the way you'll have intuitive hunches. Pay attention to these and act on them without thinking about it too much.

What is this thing called love anyway?

isness *adj.* 1) native presence of love, peace, harmony. 2) the reality of a situation or thing: *The isness of love cannot be underestimated.*

beingness *adj.* 1) the essence of a being. 2) authentic presence: *Gandhi's beingness inspired a nation.*

For some people, love is a deep sense of caring, compassion or tolerance. For others, love means joy, emotional closeness or tenderness.

When I asked people how they define love, most said that love is impossible to explain in words. You know it when you feel it, they said. There is an *is-ness* about love. I like *that* one. It's similar to the idea that there is a *being-ness* about love. Love simply is.

The experience of love cannot be made into a concept or theory, no matter how hard we try. If we try to capture love in a definition, we run the risk of turning love into a "thing" — rather than the *isness* that it is. So perhaps the less said about it the better.

A definition of what love is
will best come from what *you* feel it is.

Here are a few sentiments about love that might be helpful in your exploration of what love means to you.

♥ God is love, and love is God.

♥ In New Zealand, I've heard that the Maori people have one word for love: Aroha. It means total acceptance of another person; giving, without needing to receive anything back, and not trying to change another.

♥ Maybe there is only one kind of love—unconditional love.

♥ Love is not difficult to find; it is impossible to avoid.

♥ Love is a genuine expression of one's heart.

♥ Love is when the heart is moved, regardless of the circumstances.

♥ Love is the center of intelligence.

♥ Love is the spontaneous bursting forth of compassion.

♥ "Using words to describe love is like using a screwdriver to carve a turkey."   ~Tom Robbins

♥ "Love is the recognition of Oneness, of knowing your self as other. The Oneness is Love."   ~Eckhart Tolle

♥ A Course in Miracles says your task is not to seek love, but merely to seek and find all the barriers within yourself that you have built against it.

♥ Love is absolute acceptance of another being regardless of agreeing with them, a granting of beingness.

♥ Love is the attention and intention of understanding another's viewpoint.

♥ To love a person is to learn the song in their heart and sing it to them when they have forgotten.

♥ Shakira, age nine, says: "Love is what's in the room with you at Christmas if you stop opening presents for awhile and listen."

I am pointing you to the stillness
that is alive in the core of
your being—and inviting you
to turn your attention to *that*—
to let *that* live your life.

~Gangaji

Tell the truth faster
Have a good life

There are two mottos I love to use with
Say What You Love.
The first one is:

Tell the truth faster
(about what you love);
have a good life.

The alternative to telling the truth is to avoid saying much of
anything that is authentic for you, presumably to please others or
to only say selective pieces of your truth, as if being inauthentic
were polite.

The other motto is:

Pay now,
or pay a lot more later.

The best mind-altering drug
is truth.

~Lily Tomlin
. . . and that's the truth. plplplpp.

Sometimes we think it will be easier or less painful if we just don't say anything. But "pay now or pay a lot more later" is much like running up your credit cards. The interest builds so quickly that pretty soon it can take 20 years to pay off your bill if you haven't paid it as you go along. You may think you are saving someone disappointment or inconvenience if you don't speak up in this moment, but later it will become expensive. Guaranteed.

When you don't entrust your loved ones with your truth, inevitably you pay a lot more later in terms of hurt feelings, the time it takes to sort through misunderstandings and even lost intimacy.

Here's an example:

Clara accepts an invitation on Sunday to go to the movies with Pam on Thursday evening. On Wednesday night Clara stays up half the night caring for one of her children. Clara feels tired throughout the next day but doesn't cancel her movie plans for fear of disappointing Pam and making her angry.

At the movies, Clara falls asleep during an important scene. The friends go out for coffee afterwards and Pam says it's the best film she has seen in a long time. Clara says it was boring.

"You would have enjoyed it, had you been awake for the big love scene," Pam snaps back.

"Oh, I couldn't help it. I am so tired from getting no sleep last night. Sarah was throwing up all night, poor thing."

"You exposed me to your baby's flu!!!" Pam exclaims indignantly. "How could you do that? You know how much I hate to be sick! I can't believe you would be so thoughtless."

"I'm so sorry," Clara says, feeling dejected. "I almost cancelled, but I was afraid you'd feel so disappointed."

"Well, not as disappointed as I'll be angry if I get sick and have to miss work," Pam says.

"I was just trying to avoid hurting your feelings."

"I sure don't need any favors like that," says Pam, getting the last word.

As Clara drives home after coffee, she realizes how irritated she is at Pam for making her feel like she did something wrong, when all she wanted to do was not hurt her. The result: Clara is mad at Pam for

Never let yesterday use up today.

~R.H. Nelson

not appreciating her efforts, and Pam is upset anyway.

Had Clara spoken up about her need for rest, she could have been home and in bed early. Instead she went out, didn't enjoy the movie, and then felt the burn of her friend's temper tantrum and worries about sickness.

The upset that erupted out of that evening is an example of *pay now or pay a lot more later*. If Clara had spoken her truth about being too tired to go to the movies, she and Pam might have had to deal with a few moments of disappointment and discomfort while they rescheduled (pay now). But they would have been spared a big uncomfortable mess that ruined their entire evening (pay more later). If Clara and Pam wish to remain healthy friends, they will clear up the mess they innocently created by trying to avoid unpleasantness and will agree to speak up truthfully in future situations (pay now).

Pay now

The point is that it's better simply to speak up and tell the truth even if you think you will have to pay because someone will be disappointed, angry, or in some way reactive.

It is just as possible that *paying now* will not cost anyone anything. The person you are rescheduling with may not even be disappointed. For example, when I have spoken up in situations that I needed to change, the change often turned out to be equally as fortunate for the other person, who also preferred to do something else but was trying not to disappoint me. In cases like these, it can be hysterically funny when we don't speak up. There we are, each going along for the other and both feeling called to be somewhere else. *Pretty silly, don't you think?*

I've also had it happen when the person didn't appreciate the change of plans at first, but would later tell me that some other opportunity magically appeared that they would have missed had we stuck to the original plans. So they were grateful instead of angry.

In either case, you are doing the person a favor by rescheduling if your heart isn't in it.

Remember that <u>not</u> getting
what you want
is sometimes a wonderful
stroke of luck.

~Dalai Lama

Room for miracles

When you *tell the truth faster about what you love*, you leave room for miracles to happen for you and your loved ones. Maybe someone did you a favor once by changing plans with you. Remember, it's not their fault if you didn't do anything with the opportunity but stay home and sulk.

Next time someone changes their plans with you, even if it's last minute, thank them. Then wait to see what even-better opportunity is waiting for you. It's there. Take a breath and prepare for it to show up. Remember, follow any intuitive hunches you get without thinking about it too much.

Don't worry yourself about the negative conditioning surrounding the word truth—especially from religions and individuals who fight over who has the corner on truth. *Tell the truth faster* has nothing to do with that kind of ego or manipulation. *Telling the truth* is about saying what is inherently peaceful or harmonious for you.

You'll recognize a peacefulness within you when you say what is so without justifying it or explaining why. For example, when your best friend asks you for a favor, you might get a big ol' *yes* bursting right out of your heart, so you say, "Yes."

Or there might be some hesitation—perhaps a signal to yourself that you don't want to do what is being asked of you. As you're practicing telling the truth to yourself, take your time; you don't have to respond right away. Take a breath . . . and another . . . and patiently listen for your response. You may even answer that you will respond later. *That's okay.* Your truth may be, "Thank you and no."

Telling the truth faster can also be described as listening to that still small voice within.

Here's an example: I was short-tempered with someone one afternoon and saw her several times over the next few days without apologizing. My mental dialogue went something like this: "If you were going to apologize you should've done it already. She'll think you're weird for bringing it up so late. She's already forgotten it; you'll just bring up bad memories." *Quackquack.* However, there was a still small voice within that gently said, "There she is; you could apologize to her now. It's never too late to show kindness to someone."

It felt so good to finally apologize. To not listen to that still small voice would have kept the argument alive in my mental dialogue whenever I saw her or thought of her.

Telling the truth faster is about listening attentively to who you are and to what to do next. That's why you never have to worry about the future. When you finish the thing you were doing last, you take a moment to breathe fully, and ask, *Hmmmm*, what now? Listen for what's next. A lot can get accomplished that way—in a peaceful, non-struggle way.

It used to bug me to hear my mother say, "If you can't say something nice, don't say anything at all." Now, it seems like sage advice, especially if you re-word it for what you are creating. "If you can say something true or positive about What You Love, say that!" In all ways, let's encourage one another to Say What We Love.

Telling the truth faster gives you the opportunity to relax. Things become less complicated, simpler, more real. You no longer have to run scenarios in your mental dialogue in which you manipulate all the parts and players. "If I say this, they will say that, then. . . ." And so on.

The plan is simple. You tell your truth *about yourself,* to yourself. *Tell the truth faster* is not about your opinions of what other people should be or do. You listen to other people's truths. Believe them when they say what they love; don't think you can change them. Then, go ahead and work and play with those people you love to work and play with.

A radical perspective

I've heard a few skeptics say that SWYL is a naive and unrealistic concept. Others see amazing potential and radical implications in Say What You Love. It's all in how you look at it. In a world where it is common procedure to worry about problems, calculate how to fix problems, and complain about what the other guy is doing or not doing, yes, it appears quite radical to consider using What We Love as a reference point for making decisions.

Take, for instance, the current perspective that combat is our best option for homeland peace and security. It may seem radical to believe that Saying What You Love has the power to arouse peace or instigate change solely on its own merits. "Gosh darn it, we have real threats out there. We gotta handle those things before they get us first! No time for fluff! And love is fluff." *Isn't that what lots of people think?*

Another thing that happens is we develop a bond with our problems. We identify ourselves by our problems and then try to solve those problems as a measure of our productivity and self worth. We do this as individuals, as a nation and as a global community. Describing problems is how politicians campaign. It's

Use your thoughts wisely. Understand their power. thoughts have a tendency to become their physical equivalent. This is one of the fundamental laws of the universe.

~Dr. Christiane Northrup

how the evening news and daily newspapers relay information to capture our attention. Problem solving is also how people usually craft their lives. So, rather than creating from what they love, they use the solving of problems as a way of trying to get what they want.

This is so automatic and ingrained that it's hard to see why it doesn't work until you stop to think about it. Ask yourself: Which approach is more likely to create a positive outcome — focusing on the problem or letting a natural unforeseen solution spring forth by reorienting yourself to what you love?

Personally, when you make a choice based in a habit of solving problems, you miss an opportunity to access power. For example, maybe a young man who is unhappy, Brian, says, "I gotta get the heck out of this loser town," or Caroline decides, "I'm gonna leave the whole rat race of the city." Brian and Caroline are focusing on the problem—the loser town or the rat race city—and setting a limited goal of getting away from an unwanted situation. To access power that can unleash the best of opportunities, Brian or Caroline might ask instead: "What do I want to move toward? What do I envision for myself?"

By asking themselves questions that lead to What They Love, Brian and Caroline enter the beginning stages of power-manifesting mode. As creator beings, they are directing their attention clearly and fine-tuning their creation abilities.

Realize that you have a choice in every situation: Will you direct your attention toward envisioning What You Love to do or be? Or will you *anti-create,* a term I use to describe faulty and limited thinking focused on the opposite of what one loves?

For instance, we hear of a place called the War Room. I imagine they devise plans to make war in there. What's your guess? Yet, if it's true that we get whatever we pay attention to, and I believe that is precisely the nature of creation-energy, what results can we expect from meetings in the War Room? Certainly not peace, as our track record confirms.

I imagine a day when there is a Peace Room. I imagine that considerations of war strategies would not even be up for discussion in a Peace Room. Instead, world leaders would either have to duke it out personally (if they really thought combat would help), or they would become truly visionary and settle disputes as creator beings who focus on what the people of the world love unconditionally. If a Department of Peace received the same trillions of dollars that the War Department spends on battle ships, tanks, missiles and soldiers, the Peace Department could create amazing movement toward a tolerant and respect-

There is a saying among prospectors: "Go out searching for one thing, and that's all you'll ever find."

~Robert Flaherty

ful coexistence on Earth. Envision for a moment, how things might be organized in a Department of Peace. Meeting agendas, job titles (imagine a Secretary of Understanding, whose job it is to listen to all sides, and an Undersecretary of Gratitude, who ensures that all are valued for their special roles and talents), and visual symbols based in a language of peace would set a different tone—one that leads to peaceful results.

As creator beings, we are so powerful that we create world war simply by thinking that's our only option for security. *A bit ironic, don't you think?*

Consider your own life. Where are you using problem solving in a losing battle to try and get what you want, rather than using pure creation-energy? Consider your current job or work situation. Are you doing something you love? If you didn't need the money, would you still do the same work? How would your life be different if you did what is necessary to pay the bills, but instead of giving up on your dream, you gave it a name, a voice, and the recognition of your love?

We assume (*and it is a huge assumption!*) there will be plenty of time to do what we love later—after the important stuff of life is handled. In the meantime we figure we can do our passions on the weekends, or after we attain our goals, or certainly after we retire, right? But then there's laundry to do on the weekends, and after we reach our goals there are new goals to reach, and then arthritis or a hip replacement takes away the fun after retirement.

If we wait for a convenient time to
say and live what we love,
life will be long gone before we even know it.

Each time I intercept a worry that's brewing, and instead listen for what I love, it does feel rather radical. It's a radical shift in awareness because worry is such an automatic habit. Each time I catch the internal dialogue calculating risks, such as what it thinks it can afford so that it can decide what it can or can not buy, and then—mid-thought—switch to acknowledging what I love, it feels refreshingly radical. Even when the inner dialogue is rattling off ten perfect reasons why I can't have what I think I want, if I remain dedicated to Saying What I Love, somehow What I Love shows up. It feels like divine magic every time!

I believe in miracles. Do you?

There are only two ways to live your life: One is as though nothing is a miracle. The other is as though everything is a miracle.

~ Albert Einstein

Chapter Two

Say What You Love

In Action

Look forward to the
power of love replacing
the love of power.
Then we will know peace.

~William Gladstone

It takes a lot of effort
to <u>not</u> get what you want

When I work with clients, at some point after they list their complaints, worries and judgments, I often say, "Okay, I hear what you want and don't want. Now, tell me What You Love." For many, that's not so easy to do.

Following is one client's story. It illustrates the lack of education most of us have when it comes to getting our needs met.

Jane was a lovely woman of 40, with three great kids, perfect health, financial security, and a twenty-year relationship with her childhood sweetheart Matthew. They had a happy marriage, she said, except for the fact they rarely made love, which was the reason she came to see me. She said Matthew was an excellent father and husband—aside from the intimacy issue.

Jane reported that she usually started nagging as soon as he walked in the door. She was constantly irritated by what he did and didn't do. Her list of complaints was long.

I asked her what she liked about him. She could not

He who wants to do good
knocks at the gate;

he who loves,
finds the door already open.

~ Rabrindranath Tagore

think of anything. I asked her what she loved about him.
No response. I asked what she enjoyed about him. Still
no answer.

"Do you like his body?"

"Oh yes," she said.

"Name something about his body that you like."

"Gosh, I don't know," she replied.

"What do you love about his lovemaking style?"

"Oh, I want it to happen more often!" she said, without skipping a beat.

"I understand that. And what do you like about the
way he makes love with you?"

She shrugged.

"When you first fell in love, what attracted you to
Matthew?"

"Oh, he was *soooo* much fun!"

"Do you still think he's fun?"

"Yes, but..." and she launched right back into her
litany about what was wrong with him.

(Hmmmm. If these are the responses of someone

who considers her marriage "good," it's no surprise there's such a high divorce rate these days. It's also an example of something we all tend to do—focus on our complaints even in those areas of our lives that we consider healthy and happy.)

"Why do you guess he doesn't want to make love with you very often?"

"Probably because I always scold him. I think he thinks I don't like him."

"When was the last time you told him you enjoyed making love with him?"

"Well, I never have, but he knows I do. He must! Oh my God!!! That's awful of me, isn't it? He asks me to tell him what I enjoy in bed and to tell him what I need, but I don't know what to say, so I just don't answer. I know he knows I love him though. He better!"

I asked her how he would arrive at such knowledge.

"I am the mother of his children and I *stay* with him. *That* should account for something."

If your partner only hears from you when something is wrong and never hears about the yummy stuff you

Appreciation is a wonderful thing:
It makes what is excellent in
others belong to us as well.

~Voltaire

enjoy, it's natural for him or her to stop trying for fear of disappointing you.

For her homework, I invited Jane to create a list of things she liked, loved or appreciated about her husband. Like many women (and men), Jane wasn't able to speak about her needs because she never considered what those needs were. She rarely mentioned what she liked or what pleased her. She lived her life articulating and fine tuning what she didn't like, as if that would communicate her needs.

Jane reported that her husband was generous with gifts and vacations, and that he contributed around the house. She said she never acknowledged his good efforts because there was always something else to complain about. Mostly she feared she would lose power if she were too nice. She feared that if she stopped nagging, she would lose any hope of getting a shred of what she wanted.

This was certainly a no-win situation for Matthew. It's even sadder for Jane, because she was never able to receive his generosity of spirit or his gifts of love. He was never enough in her mind. They missed each other for twenty years.

When Jane returned for her next appointment, she was happy to report that, out of the blue, her husband had made the sweetest love with her that they had enjoyed in years.

To what did she credit this miraculous development? "To begin with, I think it's because I lightened up on the nagging. I realized how much negative energy I was putting out. I also began noticing the things I enjoy about my life and about Matthew. I started seeing the considerate little things he does that I took for granted before. I even complimented him a few times. Making the list of What I Love and appreciate still isn't exactly easy yet. But I see how quickly things change at home when I change first."

As Jane complained less and kept adding to her love-list, her husband did not comment on her changes so much as respond to them. He was more affectionate, communicative and fun to be with again, like when they were younger. Her kids noticed she was more positive, and they razzed her about it, as kids do so beautifully. She liked that.

I've asked hundreds of clients to make lists of What They Love unconditionally. It can be a tough question to answer at first. The tendency is to repeat what you just complained about, with a little rephrasing.

For example:

Jane says, "He never initiates lovemaking."

"Okay, that's what you don't want. What would you love instead?"

"He says he is too tired, and I'm tired of him not initiating."

"Okay, that's more of what you don't want. What would you love instead?"

"I want sex to happen more often!"

"That's clearly what you want. What do you *lovvve*?"

"I love to make love with him in the mornings before the kids get up."

"Perfect! That's it! What you love is very clear. How do you feel?"

"It's true. I *lovvve* making love in the mornings. But how does knowing that get me more sex in the mornings?"

"It's a bit of a mystery. We can't know exactly how it will happen for you. But if you spend your waking time musing about how much you love morning lovemaking, instead of complaining, I have a feeling you'll tell me how it works for you."

Jane reported later that she began running a bubble bath in the mornings, instead of jumping in the shower. She created space in her mornings to be sensual instead of rushing off to start her day. Guess who noticed? Before long, one thing led to another, and her husband invited himself in to play. The next time I saw Jane she was all smiles.

By acknowledging What She Loved, rather than what she did not love, Jane refocused her attention. Based on that awareness, she began setting aside time for nurturing herself in the mornings. By redirecting her energies toward what she loved, Jane created an opening for something new and wonderful to happen in her relationship with Matthew.

It's odd how we wait for the other person to give it to us—whatever it is we think we need. It's when we take ourselves out of the realm of needing, wanting and demanding that the magic happens and the thing we love has a chance to appear.

Beyond complaining

For many people, complaining is a way of life, almost an art form, it seems. Yet when we do complain, we feel helpless. We turn into victims who feel powerless to affect the source of our complaint. Even if we know enough to ask for what we like, there is often an edge in our asking, as if we're daring someone not to give us what we want. Or maybe we'll take the offering but not really receive it fully, because we're hiding behind an attitude of entitlement that blocks the joy of receiving. We act guarded, because we don't trust that our needs will be met.

Saying What You Love shifts this dynamic in a powerful way, in part because it removes the urgency and neediness you sometimes feel. As your energy is freed up, it is easier to follow intuitive leads that arise, such as Jane's thought to run a morning bubble bath. When an intuitive hunch comes to you, listen to it and follow through. Who knows what lovely miracle will happen?

And while you're listening, listen for the "yeah, but…" response—the objections, self-editing and limitations you put on those intuitive hunches, the arguments that keep those limitations in place.

I personally think we developed language because of our deep need to complain.

~Lily Tomlin

Who would you be without
the thoughts that limit you?

What would you do if you were not limited by time, money or geography? If you knew that failure was not possible, and if money was not an issue, what would you love to be doing right now?

How do you know you love something?

The SWYL way of knowing:

You know you love something when
you feel a peace within,
when there is no argument, doubt or
need to justify what you love to anyone,
including yourself.

What if I don't know what I love?

Maybe it's time to learn!

Start from wherever you are. Your clues will be what you like, want or feel you need. Don't assume that what you love is the opposite of what you complain about. Ask a few questions. Then dig deep to find the answers in your heart. For example, do you know what you like or what you want? That will point you in the right direction.

"I want a new job. My boss is unreasonable and mean. The office is on edge. It's an awful way to spend the day."

"Okay. If this boss were reasonable instead of unreasonable, would you like this job?"

"I like the benefits. The hours are fair. The pay is good. Yeah, if the boss was decent, I'd prefer to stay actually."

"Okay, good. This is an easy one. I hear that you love great hours, benefits and pay, in a harmonious environment. Is that accurate?"

"Yes, it's true. I love great hours, benefits, pay and harmony."

When you know you only have one thing to stand on it's easy to speak.

~ Byron Katie

Focusing your attention on those things you love about your job creates far more power for a harmonious outcome for you than merely complaining about what you hate about your job.

The possibilities for miracles are endless. You may get a new job, or your current job situation may improve before your very eyes. You need not worry about how the harmony is going to manifest. You only have to acknowledge what you love.

Be honest if you think you *should* want something other than what you love—such as the "reasonable" or "practical" thing, or the thing that will impress others or not ruffle their feathers. This is not a matter of not knowing What You Love. It is a conflict. You are choosing something other than What You Love. As long as you think you should do something—for any reason other than love—you will not be able to hear very well What You Love.

If you decide to acknowledge What You Love, I have a feeling you will be pleasantly surprised with how easy it is to know What You Love.

Albert Einstein once said, "When the solution is simple, God is answering." That's how love feels. Love is simple. Peaceful.

As long as you have certain desires about how it ought to be, you can not see how it is.

~ Ram Das

Tag. You're it!

How do you respond to someone
after they tell you What They Love?

When someone Says What They Love, it is not a request or a demand on you. You do not have to love it too. You do not even have to like it. And you certainly are not obliged to figure out how to get them what they love (unless you notice that you would love to do that).

When someone Says What They Love, it is a love truth. Simply hear it. Receive the gift of truth. That's it.

Okay, you now have a choice to say what you love if you care to. What You Love does not have to be the same as what someone else loves. *Imagine that!* (It's the end of being the kind of "nice" that keeps you walking on egg shells, and it's the beginning of being authentically kind to yourself and others.)

Lets say you describe what you love about this year's vacation plans. Then your partner says what she loves. Saying what you each love diffuses the power struggle in any situation, because you can argue about choices, facts, opinions and behaviors, but you can't argue with what someone loves. It's ridiculous. Think ice cream. If you love chocolate ice cream, it would be insane to think your partner does not love you if she loves strawberry ice cream. It's hopeless to argue with what someone loves unconditionally, because it is simply so. It's not personal.

How would your life be different
if you simply heard what other people love?

There would be no more pressure to perform, no anxiety about disappointing one another, no more compromises that hurt. There would be no need to second-guess hidden agendas, implications or assumptions.

Here's how it might work:

John says over dinner how much he loves the opera. All you have to do is hear him. That's it. Did you notice he did not make it an invitation? So it's simple. How do you know that all you have to do is hear him? He did not ask you to go with him or to do anything.

If John says, "I would love for you to join me at the opera," now there is an invitation on the table. So you check in with yourself about What You Love. Do you love opera? Do you love just to be wherever John is? If your answer is yes, then your response goes accordingly. Now it's *your* turn to say What You Love. Or if you don't love going to the opera with John, say something like, "Thank you, but no."

You never have to worry about morality in SWYL because it is built into the system. If John is married to someone else, and you have any inkling that an opera date would be troublesome for you, him, or the wife, then it doesn't fit the SWYL criteria of no argument, justification, or doubt. You might say you *want* to go. But that's not being true to the SWYL principle, because it's *not* true that you love to go unconditionally. So it's simple to know what to do.

How would your life be different if you simply let other people hear what you love?

There would be no more trying to manipulate others into doing what you want. No more holding back what you love for fear of hurting people. Freedom! What You Love is not about other people. Please understand that what *you* love is not a betrayal or disrespect of others.

Good. Say What You Love. Unconditionally.

Tag. You're it!

*Thank you
for telling me
what you love,
because that's
the only way
I'm really ever going
to know you.
And I love to know you.
~love,
your friend*

Breathe love

Connected breathing is as valuable as gold when it comes to making you feel wealthy and peaceful. Luckily, your breath is free! Breath is the one thing you have for your whole life.

Your connected and full breath fills you with peace and relaxes you. Every aspect of your being functions better when you breathe fully and connectedly. Your heart rate, digestion and elimination, mental perceptions, communication, intimacy, energy, vitality and even your intelligence are increased when you breathe fully.

When your breath does not expand below the upper chest area, you'll feel prone to worry and anxiety, no matter how much wealth or health you have.

When your breath is shallow, you are under the spell of the *machine mind* of worry, judgment and stress. It's as if you're stuck on automatic pilot, working for your machine mind 24 hours a day, seven days a week, with no chance of parole. *Uhhrraaa*, without a break. No time off for nights, weekends or vacations.

However, once you breathe fully and connectedly, you break the emotional and mental bondage of the automated

The Connected Breath
To inhale and exhale in a relaxed flow. Take a relaxed full breath into the belly, pause for just a moment, then exhale in a relaxed flow, pause for just a moment, and so on.

machine mind. Breathing fully and connectedly gives you a sort-of *Get Out of Jail Free* card.

It's a beginning. Breathing is always the beginning. And with practice, full connected breathing can also be the breath you default to when you're suddenly shocked or hurt. You rise above the playing field, so you can see clearly where to move next. You gain flexibility and options. You have clearer access to your innate intelligence and wisdom.

When your breath is habitually shallow, you can't even imagine the peace that full connected breathing can give you. The pervasive anxiety fueled by shallow breathing is no fun. You can't help but automatically distrust brighter options when your breath is shallow.

In general, fear will fill any void created by *not* living What You Love. Fear also will result from shallow, unconnected breathing.

When you breathe fully, it's as if your authentic intelligence and natural creativity get switched on. It's actually difficult to be afraid when you are in that space. The body/mind is naturally relaxed.

Acknowledging and Saying What You Love is easier when you breathe fully. You aren't so afraid of what other people think

Fear can fill up any void created by not living What You Love.

of you, and you don't let judgments, yours or others', deter you from shining your love.

In fact, to put a little spin on something Anais Nin once said, "The day may come when your fear of living life the way you love it will be less than the fear of *not* living your life the way you love it."

I love that you know you have a choice when it comes to feeling fear or love, feeling just okay or feeling fabulous, and just getting by or going for it. It's simply up to you how much joy and freedom you love unconditionally.

No matter who you are or what your life looks like, you can choose to breathe fully. And it's free, which means it's cheaper and more effective than self-medicating behaviors like zombie television-watching, overeating, compulsive shopping, over-doing drugs and alcohol, smoking, worrying, or blaming the other guy.

Well, that's my commercial endorsement for breathing! Just remember, breathing is free! "And *free*," said businessman Tom Peterson, "is a *very* good price."

SWYLisms

♥ You are the best source of knowing What You Love.

♥ You are the voice of What You Love. No one can tell you what you love more than you.

♥ Live as if other people love to know What You Love, even if they appear not yet aware that they love that.

♥ Saying What You Love is best expressed in the positive. For instance: "I love having a home," rather than, "I love not being homeless." (Hint: If you're trying to SWYL with the word "not" in there, it's probably not Saying What You Love.)

♥ Though SWYL is likely the most powerful manifesting tool you will ever use, there is still no benefit to Saying What You Love as a ploy to reach a particular outcome or goal. How something manifests is none of your concern. Say What You Love for the peacefulness and sanity that being truthful gives you. What evolves is the miracle.

- When you SWYL, you're magnetic, so all you really have to do is receive the abundance that's all around you. Go ahead and follow any intuitive hunches you have, without analyzing them too much.

- There are no certain things that you should or should not love. Shoulds and should nots—also called *shoulding*—are neither love nor loving.

- Say What You Love unconditionally, without argument or justification.

- If you are justifying or arguing, you have not yet found What You Love.

- If you feel pressure, anxiety or doubt, you have not yet found What You Love.

- When you Say What You Love, you feel a peace that is calming, simple and uncomplicated.

- Love is innocent. Love needs no justification to be valid.

- Love is. You are love. And so are we.

- SWYL does not ask you to believe that SWYL works.

- Love is your native intelligence.

- There is something to love in every single moment.

- Go ahead and notice. There is something to love right this minute.

- Discovering that you love to know what other people love unconditionally can release you from a lifelong habit of imposing your expectations on, and thereby rudely manipulating, the very people you say you love most. Thus SWYL is a path of freedom and kindness.

- If you Say What You Love today and it feels good, feel free to do so again tomorrow.

Chapter Three

Don't Believe
Everything You Think

Dew knot trussed yore
spell chequer two fined
awl yore mistakes.

~Brendan Hills

Change the channel

Just like the television that's on in the next room, the thoughts in our minds run continuously in the background, whether or not we pay attention to them. We naturally assume these thoughts belong to us, but they are not personal. Most of them have been sponsored by family members or authorities. If you listen, you can hear the attitudes, beliefs and judgments that belonged to your parents, teachers and religious representatives.

These thoughts may make you feel guilty, defensive or responsible for improving yourself in some way. Until you begin to verify the reality of those thoughts, you probably react to them as if they are your own. They're in *your* brain, right? Yet, the only thoughts that belong to you are the ones you reach up, take hold of in the moment and claim as your own.

You can be cooking in the kitchen while the television plays in the background with commercials, news, movies, cartoons, soap operas and game shows. One after another. There are announcements of coming attractions to hook you into tuning in next week, same time, same station. That's what the machine mind does also: It gives you coming attractions to worry about, fix and to dread, providing endless hours of entertainment.

Just as watching television can consume your entire day, so can the fear and worry in your machine mind. The machine mind will trick you into believing that its endless stream of fear and worry will help you cope. Yet fear and worry do not help you handle matters more efficiently, easily or brilliantly. Knowing what you love does.

When you see a show on TV that you don't like because it's scary or boring, you know you can change the channel, right? Good. It's the same with your thoughts. If you don't love the mind-shows that make you fearful, anxious or bored, change the station to what you do love.

In the middle of a problem,
chaos or crisis, ask yourself:
"What would I love right now?"
and then,
What do I love?

SAY WHAT YOU LOVE *Unconditionally*

It's only a parade

The mind beams an endless stream of thoughts. Millions of them a day. Where the heck do they all come from? You can sit right where you are and watch the thoughts arise out of nowhere and speed across your mental telescreen. Yep, there's another one now. Oh, and another one. And another one.

The thoughts arise as intelligence and flashes of insight or as judgments, anxiety, desperation, worry, self-consciousness, vanity, shoulds, can'ts, and guilt-fests. The thoughts can be contradictory, not based in reality, and mean-spirited toward yourself, and you'll still probably believe them.

What if you chose which thoughts to believe and act on and didn't respond to the rest? If you did not take the thoughts parading through your mind so personally, perhaps you could experience them like you do a movie or radio show. Though some people scream at their televisions from time to time, mostly we watch with a detached surety that what is on TV is not personal or real. For instance, when the Starship Enterprise gets shipwrecked in Klingon territory, you don't call 911 for help or write your congressman to demand better space ships, right? They'd

Fear is simply there sometimes. Judgments, worry, doubt arise.

Who would you be without a story that it's yours?

~The Work

> You cannot depend on your eyes
> when your imagination is
> out of focus.
>
> ~Mark Twain

cart you off to the looney bin. It's a fiction and we know that. Actors and movie props.

Yet, unless you're a natural meditator (a great resource for discerning the reality of your thoughts), you probably believe that the thoughts or movies in your brain represent the truth, the reality of the situation. They seem so real. Surely it's right to act on those thoughts and resolve them. Isn't it? Well, no. Not necessarily.

How would your life be different if you recognized that ninety-nine percent of your thoughts were reruns of other thoughts, shadows of nightmares, or recycled hearsay from other fearful machine minds? Who would you be in your life if your mind came with the same disclaimer used by those psychic hotlines—"Intended for entertainment purposes only"?

If you want to have some fun, try being conscious of such a disclaimer for a day, or even a half-hour, or five minutes. You might discover peace in that moment, and that you have more energy for the thoughts that inspire you.

Your Inner Guide

What if you had a built-in mechanism that could tell you which of your millions of thoughts were based in love and worth addressing with your time and energy? You do!

Everyone has a natural mechanism for knowing, even you!

Some people get a rush of goose bumps, usually on their arms, neck or head, that signals to them the truth or accuracy of a given thought, feeling, or situation. For some people, the built-in mechanism is a sudden thump of knowingness in the gut.

The mechanism that everyone has, or could have if they developed awareness of it, is the one experienced as peace. Some people may find this mechanism unbelievable, but don't *bah humbug* it too prematurely. It goes something like this:

- ♥ Any thought that does not generate a sense of peace within you is an illusion.

- ♥ Any thought that would have you feel less than unconditional love for yourself is an illusion.

- ♥ Any thought that makes you strike out defensively or justify yourself is an illusion.

- ♥ Thoughts and feelings that summon a sense of peace within you are the real deal. Act on those.

- ♥ When you acknowledge What You Love unconditionally, without justification, reservation or argument, you will experience a sense of peace within you.

All that we are arises with our thoughts. With our thoughts, we make our world.

~Buddha

Saying What You Love is your surest, fail-safe mechanism for knowing which thoughts are worth believing and moving forward on. With millions of thoughts passing by, most of them derogatory and negative, why would you believe just any ol' thing you think?

The longest journey you will ever take is the 18 inches from your head to your heart.

~anonymous

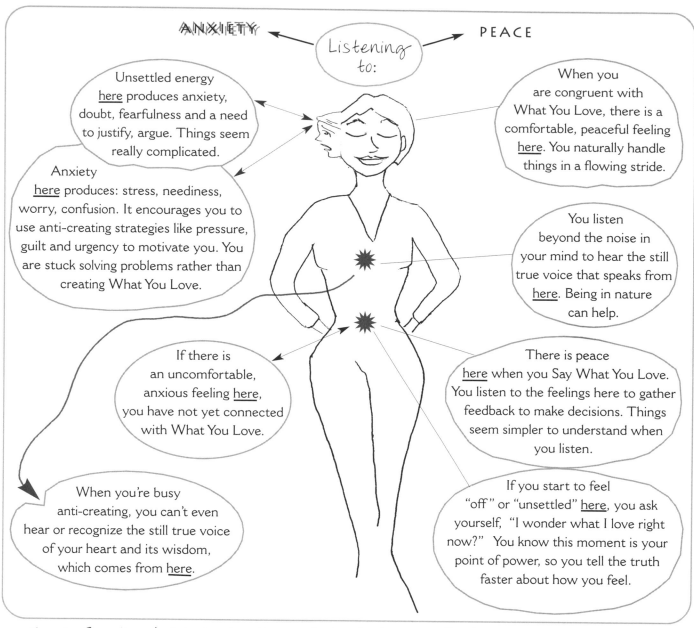

Tune in. Breathe. Get in touch with your body. Listen. The feedback you notice is priceless.

When it hurts, inquire—verify the cause

When you have painful thoughts that urge you to react to their drama, inquire into the reality of them. Write down the thought, belief or story that is causing you to feel bad. Then ask yourself the questions posed by Byron Katie in what she calls THE WORK. Ask the questions, then listen for the answers that *arise from the heart*.

You can do it right now. Think of a person or situation that upsets you and write it down. For example: Robert should stop telling me what to do.

Ask yourself these questions:

Is it true?

Can I really know that it is true?

How do I react when I think that thought or believe that concept?

Can I see a reason to drop that thought, belief or story? *(And you're not being asked to drop it, only if you can see a reason to drop it.)*

All war belongs on paper.

~Byron Katie

Can I think of one reason to keep the thought or belief, a reason that does not cause stress?

Who would I be without that thought, belief or story?

Then, do a turn-around.
Robert should stop telling me what to do.
changes to:
I should stop telling me what to do.
(Can you find the places in your life where *you* are telling you what to do?)

Another turn-around is:
I should stop telling Robert what to do. (Even if you're not doing it out loud, you're certainly telling him in your thoughts.)

This is a good turn around. Perhaps you believed it was okay for you to tell Robert what to do but not okay for him to tell you.

The turn-around uncovers a hypocrisy within *you*, the thing you thought *other* people could or should be doing, the thing you could start doing.

Re-examine all that you have been told. . . dismiss that which insults your soul. Whatever satisfies your soul is truth.

~Walt Whitman

Katie teaches that the turn-arounds reveal our own advice for happiness, a prescription for our own well-being. Besides, if we think it's so easy for Robert to do what we are asking, perhaps we can begin closer to home, *with self*. Start there.

For more detail on this life-enhancing and peace-making inquiry process, read *Loving What Is*, by Byron Katie with Stephen Mitchell.

*Let him that would
move the world,
first move himself.*

~Socrates

There's no need to justify, prove, or sell what you love

When you Say What You Love, you no longer need to justify yourself. Proving your point of view or selling your perception become unnecessary, even pointless. In fact, one way of identifying if you are not Saying What You Love is to notice whether you find yourself justifying, explaining, proving or selling. We are so accustomed to asking why or explaining why that we consider it a natural part of conversation, much like the habitual, "Hi. How are you?"

If I ask you why you love to cuddle up in a big blanket with a cup of warm tea in the evening, your machine mind will go into action to find the reasons why. The mind is so creative, and so happy to have a job, that it will come up with half a dozen reasons for justifying why you love the blanket and warm tea in the evening.

If you answer my question with a reason, you essentially give me permission to argue with you and your reasons. Let's say you respond with, "The evening's a good time to reflect on the day and think." I could counter, "Morning has been proven to be a more productive time for thinking in ten million scientific studies. Why do you do your thinking in the evening?" Now, your mind begins coming up with answers to that question.

Now musing about your reasons might make for entertaining and productive conversations. But if you are sharing with me What You Love, then you need offer no reasons justifying why you love what you love. If I ask you why anyway, your response, minus the justifying, might be: "I don't know" or "I love to reflect in the evenings." And what's that? It's another SWYL! It needs no justification. I can't argue with What You Love.

Saying What You Love does not invalidate other interesting realities or opportunities for you. It's not about putting your head in the sand. SWYL does not mean others must bend to fit your whims. SWYL is clear communication. You are simply noticing and Saying What You Love.

Feeling worthy is not required

Getting what you want or need usually entails feeling worthy enough to receive it. Luckily, this is not a requirement for Saying What You Love.

Imagine Eugena, a middle-aged woman who has prayed for her husband to stop beating her, but who also feels she deserves the abuse. All her wishing and hoping for the abuse to stop are useless because she feels unworthy of better treatment. Plus, wanting something to stop is not as powerful as visioning what you do want, and then refining that to what you love.

If we can teach one another that loving something is a greater vehicle for change than wanting something, then maybe even battered women will be able to heal themselves into safety. It may seem too much for Eugena to believe she deserves the beatings to stop. But if she makes a silent note that she enjoys someone being kind or gentle with her, perhaps a change will begin to take root within her psyche that will allow her to accept a safe space.

Eugena never even has to say, "I want kindness for myself." It's enough to say, "I love my neighbor's kindness" or "I love kindness." From there, she can cultivate a feeling of safety.

You do not need to feel worthy to practice Saying What You Love. You don't have to feel deserving to SWYL. You simply must be a reporter of what you love. Your love for yourself will grow from that experience.

No effort or seeking is necessary. Simply report what you love.

How is it possible to live without

knowing what we love unconditionally?

Because

problems

are

attractive,

mesmerizing

distractions.

Better than immunity

The moment you choose love,
hell vanishes.

~Emmanuel

Saying What You Love does not make you immune from the dramatic events of life. Saying What You Love does give you access to the calm eye inside the storm. From that calm place, you don't have to worry about how to produce an outcome or overcome impossibilities. You simply Say What You Love in the moment.

Follow any hunches you receive. Don't worry about looking silly or different. You are a creator being. Verbally or silently, Say What You Love, unconditionally, in all situations.

When the house is burning down, it's not the best time to sit around complaining about the terrible things that always happen to you; you could burn down too! Notice that you love having legs to walk on or a wheelchair to carry you outside. Love that you have a voice to call for help, or that you have neighbors who have a telephone to call 911. Something dramatic is happening; that's true. What do you love about who you are in that situation? Identify what you love as you move through the experience.

Whatever the occasion, it is up to you to notice what you love in that moment. The parents are aging. Stocks drop.

Dinners are burnt. Husbands leave. There is no money for gas to drive to work. The teacher is unfair with grades. Situations happen. Okay, now, say what you do love unconditionally. No time is better than right now.

Try Saying What You Love even in high drama situations. Notice how Saying What You Love transforms not only your experience of what's happening, but what to do about it, and how the future looks.

Chapter Four

Creator Comics

The statistics on sanity are that
one out of every four Americans
is suffering from some form of
mental illness. Think of your
three best friends. If they're okay,
then it's you.

~Rita Mae Brown

The downward spiral of anti-creating

These are three, fairly familiar stages of anti-creating:

The Clean Slate: You start out with pure innocence and naivete. A feeling that "of course *this* will work. Why wouldn't it? All I have do is work really hard, or get a degree, or marry into the right family, or write out my 'wants' list, or do my affirmations, or pray or chant om or do some other thing 'they' say will breed success. Then it will all work out."

Rude Awakenings: It's not happening. Something is missing in the plan. But what? There's a feeling of "I did what was expected but it's not working. Quick! Find out what went wrong. Fix it! Try something else, back paddle before totally sinking. *Avoid* failure."

The Victimization Cycle: After your innocence is burned away by the rude awakenings, you're left with a feeling of "what's wrong with *me*?" It starts with a little self-doubt, which rattles your confidence. This can quickly spiral downward, disintegrating your remaining self-esteem, then spawn a mistrust of everything you used to believe in. Anti-creation backlash: *pretty darn ugly.*

When the victim cycle kicks in, you have more than one task on your plate to manage. Instead of simply manifesting the thing you originally wanted, you have a few "problems" you have to solve first, such as low self-esteem, poverty consciousness and a victim mentality. People can spend their whole lives trying to fix mistaken perceptions that resulted from anti-creating. How can you fix something that was not broken in the first place?

No matter how real these perceptions may feel to you, they do not actually block your creations unless you believe them. Focusing on them will only further distract you from pure creating and delay your successes.

This was Terri's situation.

Terri had a dream of selling her all-natural cookie recipe to a particular nationwide cookie chain. Year after year she fell deeper into despair because she assumed she lacked the discipline and self-confidence to follow through on her dream. This led her to question her commitment, her talent, and her worthiness. She spent countless hours trying to improve her confidence and to develop the right discipline so that she could one day materialize her dream. But it was never enough. She felt

Politics is the art of
looking for trouble—
to find it,
misdiagnose it, and
then to misapply
the wrong remedies.

~Groucho Marx

broken. She constantly berated herself for not getting it together.

I asked Terri if she had any experience in the corporate arena.

"None," she said.

"Have you ever written a business plan?"

"No," she replied.

"Do you know *how* to pitch a cookie recipe deal to a big chain? Do you know *who* to contact, *what* to expect, *what* to offer, *how* to present your idea?"

"No," she replied again. "*Ohhhh*," she said, as the light bulb came on. "I don't have the hands-on experience for what I've been trying to do."

Her problem was *not* lack of discipline. She actually had enormous focus and dedication in every area of her life. Her main mistake was only in *where* she directed her focus and efforts. In the rush to fix her "faults," it hadn't occurred to her that what she needed for success was a little education and some specific experience.

She redirected her attention from trying to gain more confidence and discipline into learning how to play in big business. That one shift in perception changed her entire relationship to her dream. Also, simply switching to that perception instantaneously eliminated her victim story and the belief that she was defective.

When we fail to create what we intended because we are applying anti-creation strategies, we usually feel betrayed or we get mad, or we make even more mistakes. Ultimately, we become awfully hard on ourselves as we imagine all new character flaws and personality defects and then devise intricate ways to correct them, hide them, or hide *from* them.

This chapter of comics pokes some fun at the many ways we anti-create and illustrates how to create using the purest power.

First, a word of explanation. You may be surprised to find that one of the characters in these comics is God. I believe that God has an unconditional sense of humor, and that God loves it when we laugh and play in life. Although the God who stars in the following comics may not be the God of your current understanding, or of your religious upbringing, you *will* meet a God who loves and respects you unconditionally.

The following comics are all
fictitiously true and honestly false.

Any similarities to actual events
is probably universal.

As you read along
look for those places where Mary
forgets to notice what she loves.

ENJOY!

OK GOD,

I would like a soul mate now.

Please send me a wonderful man ...

...who is gorgeous, romantic, charming, financially independent, intelligent, has a great sense of humor, is fun, caring, sensitive, but strong, spontaneous, a good listener, not a couch potato, is tan and athletic, but not a sports fanatic, <u>and</u> someone who ...

... loves his mother, loves and wants kids, <u>and</u> who supports women's rights and respects my opinions, adores me, <u>and</u> is generous, spiritual, emotionally available, sensuous. Oh, <u>and</u> talks stuff thru, helps around the house but also gets us a maid, loves our kids, puts the seat down <u>and</u> changes the TP roll. <u>And</u> anything I forgot to add. OK. that's it.
~ YES, <u>I</u> <u>DESERVE</u> <u>ALL</u> <u>THIS</u> ~
AMEN. Thank you God!
Oh. And a June wedding would be terrific.
Amen.

It's the happiest day of my life!

Thank you God ...

He's EVERYTHING I asked for.

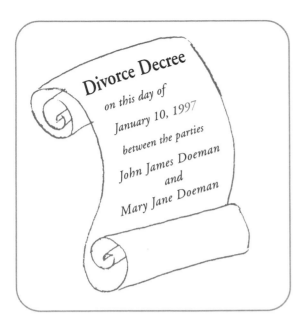

Divorce Decree
on this day of
January 10, 1997
between the parties
John James Doeman
and
Mary Jane Doeman

HEY GOD!!
<u>WHAT</u> happened?!!!
Was my list <u>too</u> long? Or was I supposed to make a list of what <u>I</u> <u>DON'T</u> <u>want</u>? Because...I'd give up some of the help around the house for someone who is

<u>NOT</u> AN ALCOHOLIC.

Amen.

...p.s.,
could he at least be good to our kids, and be a kind and romantic man, who can hold down a steady job?
OK. Thanks.
Amen.

He's perrrfect.

...Ask for less, get more?

OK. I guess That's how it works.

SAY WHAT YOU LOVE *Unconditionally*

This Divorce
is final on
this day of
June 10, 1999
between the parties
James John Joeman
and
Mary Jane Joeman

DEAR GOD,
  I hate to be <u>sooo</u> hard to please,
but when I said
        r o m a n t i c, . . .
I <u>MEANT</u> <u>WITH ME</u> !!!!!

Not with his secretary
  and every other floozy
    around this town.
  What is the problem with getting
                what I want?!!!

OK GOD, what about . . .
  . . . not bad to look at, can
keep a steady job, comes home
after work, is sober at least
      a year, and is
      monogamous.
              <u>With me.</u>
      ok. that's plenty.
    That's all I really need.
                amen.

I didn't ask for this,
Did I? He comes home
alright, but he won't
let me go out
with my friends.
He dictates
what I wear.
He's a paranoid,
penny pinching,
controlling, obsessive,
nightmare! Arrrrgghhhhhh!!!

GOD!
ARE YOU TRYING
TO TELL ME THERE
ARE NO GOOD MEN
OUT THERE?

I don't
even want to try again.
I GIVE UP!!!

. . . as if <u>that</u> will help

When our perfect prayers, wish lists and best-laid plans don't seem to work out, we naturally feel disappointed and just ask for less, as if *that* will help.

When we get more than we bargained for, for instance, we end up with an alcoholic mate, or a Don Juan, we think we should have been more specific about what we don't want, as if *that* will help.

When affirmations, wish lists and prayers fall short, we'll try just about anything to get our mojo back. We'll downsize our needs, we'll compromise our wants, and we'll resort to any other worthless anti-creation strategy we can think of, as if *that* will help.

Your attitude,
your intention
and What You Say You Love,
count.

What you ask for,
all the statements you make,
are prayers to God.*
Even the anti-creating statements.

The attitudes and intentions you choose
are jewels that set energies into motion.
They can create gold,
or garbage.

*The God or Creative Force of your understanding.

Whether you think that you
can, or that you can't,
you are usually right.

~Henry Ford

God hears you

God does not judge by the same morality code we were taught to believe God uses. God is love. God does not judge your efforts right or wrong or pass / fail. Humans do. And painfully.

God recognizes you as a creator being. One with power to choose love, compassion and peace, in the time frame and ways you feel are best for your path.

Given that, why would God question you or your choices, or meddle with your growth process?

You may feel cheated that God won't just fill in the missing details of what you, in retrospect, *really* meant to say in order to manifest what you *wanted*. Apparently, God doesn't see a reason to override your free will. God figures you know best what you need.

God hears what you mean precisely and trusts you completely to experience your existence exactly the way that best serves you and your growth.

There is a saying, "You get what you pay attention to."

This simply means that what you observe today
about the people and things in your world, and
what you choose to spend your time talking
about, sets the field for what you will see and
experience and get to talk about again tomorrow.

"Hey, Mary.
If you weren't so
interested in identifying
and defending against jerks,
what else would you
be doing?"

If you don't want to interact with jerks, especially in your own mind, (like you do when you think about them all the time), then <u>what</u> qualities <u>would</u> you love to think about instead?

I don't know.

Here's the thing, we become
so comfortable saying what we:

don't like,

don't want,

don't need,

can't stand,

wish were better,

wish were different,

etc. . . .

. . . that we completely lose track of what we like, love and appreciate.

We assume there is more power in complaining.

Well, there *is* tremendous power in complaining. You were right (unfortunately)! You'll get just as much to complain about the next day.

However complaining does not have the power to give you joy. Saying What You Love does.

"Mary,
What would be the opposite
of jerk qualities?"

*We begin from wherever
we are. Sometimes, the
most we can do is start
with the opposite of our
current complaint in hopes
that this gives us a hint
of what we do love.*

Opposite?
Hmmmmmmm.
I guess . . .
thoughtful,
considerate,
respectful.

EXCELLENT!

Now, have you noticed anyone
matching that description
~ any real person ~ man, woman or child,
or even a fictional character in a movie or book,
someone acting thoughtful, considerate, or
respectful, say, in the last few days?

Nope.

SAY WHAT YOU LOVE *Unconditionally*

You betcha **THAT COUNTS** !!

. . . <u>IF</u> you notice!

And <u>if</u> you take the opportunity
to give it your attention and appreciation
. . . like maybe mentioning it casually
to a girlfriend or by acknowledging
it in your prayers.

OH.

... my sister has the most wonderful husband! Mark heard about this terminally ill little boy who wanted to be an NBA player. The Make-A-Wish people wanted to take him ...

... to some big league games. And Mark! what a great guy! He gave his last 4 games to that little boy. And, the team is <u>winning</u> these days ...

... so it's a real sacrifice for him to miss! He is so amazingly thoughtful and generous. I love that!

God's
speedy reply

Bless
her heart.
Mary is interested
in thoughtfulness,
generosity, consideration
and respect.
Good. Wish granted.
Send her a flurry of
random acts of
kindness and
plenty of
thoughtfulness.

And, add
those qualities
to Mary's list
of what she loves
in a soul mate.

SAY WHAT YOU LOVE *Unconditionally*

You get to choose

Whenever you pay attention to what you like,
love or appreciate, you win. Have you noticed?

Whenever you give attention to what you
dislike, worry or complain about,
you feel unpeaceful or helpless,
or angry, betrayed, victimized,
. . . or really alone.
Have you ever noticed that?

Remember that you have a choice.

You can
Say What You Love
Unconditionally

Power manifesting

In a creative process, whether you want a mate, a scooter, or to travel the world, align yourself with pure creation power by Saying What You Love.

The specifics of your wish can include everything you ever wanted, *as long as,* the wishes are also What You Love unconditionally, without justification or argument.

Soul mate magic

Let's take Mary's soul mate situation. When she notices what she loves, for instance, generosity and kindness, *those* qualities become part of her official soul mate wish list. She glows whenever she noticing those qualities, so they go straight to God's ear and become part of and activates her *real* creation list.

As she goes through her day, she notices What She Loves. She sees a man affectionately holding his sweetheart while waiting in line ahead of her at the movies. She thinks to herself, "I love affectionate men who cuddle in public."

Make your sacred
soul mate wish list by
going through your day
noticing the qualities you love
in people, about relationships
and relating styles.
That's pure creation power.

The qualities you love
unconditionally are like
little rocketships that go
straight from your heart
to God's ears to be
instantly placed on
your divine wish list.

A point to remember: No matter how tempting it might be, don't add thoughts like, "But what's up with those high water pants?" or "I sure wouldn't want such a nerdy guy."

What happens when you add things like that to SWYL? Yep, they go right on your creator wish list just the same as the affectionate cuddler does. It's that darn habit of constant criticism that clouds your creative power.

You don't have to like all of any one person's qualities in order to appreciate their juicy ones. *Do* pay your attention to What You Love, and simply bless the parts that you're not crazy about. It's not your job to fix their "imperfections," dress them better, or even to agree with them. And it certainly doesn't help your creation process to think that it is. So bless the less-than-what-you-love things, and move on to more SWYL.

By the way, please don't be jealous of your best friend's amazing *so called* one-of-a-kind mate. Create your own instead by celebrating every quality you love about him or her. You do this simply by Saying What You Love. Those qualities will go straight on your soul mate creation list.

What you perceive in others you are strengthening in yourself.

~A Course in Miracles

Get very excited for all the people who have and be and do what you love. Be inspired and SWYL immediately!

When affirmations don't work, it ain't pretty

An affirmation is a popular tool for wishing something into manifestation. You usually use them when you don't yet have what you're affirming. For example, when you're feeling vulnerable about holding onto your job, you might say over and over again, "I am confident, and the boss needs me."

Playing around with affirmations that aren't based on What You Love is like a round of no-win badminton with your worst enemy. You serve up something positive and inspiring. Your machine mind opponent fires back enough negative ammo to win the game and match. Your machine mind knows all the tender little places where you are weak and vulnerable to attack.

Service anyone?

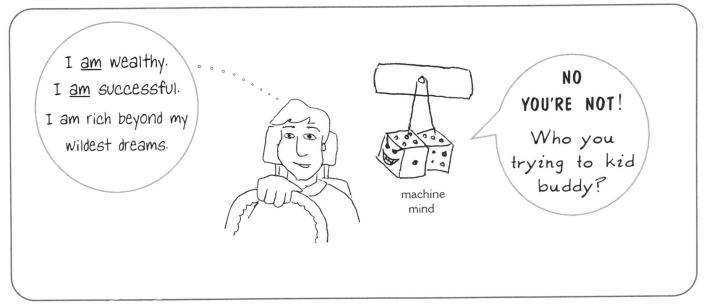

SAY WHAT YOU LOVE *Unconditionally*

I am confident, fearless and powerful. People <u>listen</u> to me. I am promoted right thru the glass ceiling!

Don't break any glass! If they listen to you, the poor company would probably fold. Just be nice. Don't rock the boat. Don't get fired.

machine mind

I now attract my ideal 3-bedroom home with a large yard.

For the price you can afford, it will probably be built over a toxic dump.

machine mind

The missing ingredient
in any affirmation,
goal, or dream
that hasn't come true yet
is What You Love
unconditionally.

When you use affirmations like these
that trigger an automatic machine mind response,
all you do is <u>affirm</u> that you're a liar.
So every time you say them,
you either confirm you're lying or that your affirmation
is not true.

To manifest something you
love enough to create,
take the chance and
Say What You Love unconditionally.

Then, follow any intuitive leads that come to you—
without thinking about it too much.

Chapter Five

As You Wish

It takes as much imagination to create debt as to create income.

~Leonard Orr

Simon says

Remember the childhood game Simon Says? You had to do whatever the leader (Simon) said, but only if they put the words "Simon says" before the order. You were penalized if you followed any commands that did not include the "Simon says" phrase.

Well, games like that still play out in the adult world, only commands other than "Simon says" commit you to attitudes, problems, and situations that might not be your first choice if you were choosing consciously.

There are people who say, "Like clockwork, I always get three colds a year." And they do! How's that possible year after year? It happens because the body and mind are linked, and because they feel a sense of ownership of that specific outcome. They have no doubt they will get those three colds, so it happens just that way. Imagine your power if you had that kind of certainty about everyday things like having plenty of health, wealth, success, centeredness, and loving relationships.

You get different results if you lack confidence in, or ownership of, your beliefs and statements. For instance, when you say,

Your word is your wand

~Francis Shovel Shinn

"How come I never get to go someplace warm in winter?" (victim statement) or "Boy, no one ever gives *me* a free house to live in on the beach" (stating a lack as a fact).

Remember, your language determines if you'll get gold or garbage for your efforts.

Have you ever thought, "If only I had a magic wand, I would _____"? Well, you do have a magic wand of sorts—your words. The only thing is, unless you understand the power of your manifesting wand and how it works, the wand is invisible to you, seems useless or, worse, can seem to work against you.

Your words are your wand's command, so be clear and precise with your language. There is a hidden power in your spoken words and attitudes that can work against your conscious desires. Also, remember to look up your favorite creation words in the Glossary or dictionary to double-check that they are creating gold, not garbage, for you.

Here are some common and not-so-common expressions that reflect the power of words and how they begin a contract that binds you. What will you purchase with your words today?

*If you say so.
*Oh, I don't care.

You get what you pay your attention to. 100%.

*It can't be done.

*Whatever. Whatever you say.

*Be careful what you ask for, you could get it.

*Argue for your limitations and you get to keep them.

*Your word is your bond, whether your fingers are
  crossed behind your back or not.

*Say the word.

*Your word is a contract. It buys gold or garbage.

*Ask and you shall receive.

*You get what you pay attention to.

*As you wish.

*I am.
  (Whenever you add the words "I am" to any
  statement, it gains special creative power. "I am" is
  a proclamation. Do you wish to proclaim, "I am
  exhausted" (or bored or starving)? Or would it be
  truer to say that the body requires rest, sleep or
  food? How many people who suffer from Chronic
  Fatigue started out by saying, "I am so exhausted.")

Find the thought that is
your greatest oppressor,
the log causing the jam —
straighten it.
The river will flow again.

~Francis Shovel Shinn

The power of prayer

Prayer is often thought of as a communication with God, whether it be a plea for guidance or a request for help meeting a material need. The act of prayer delivers our intentions and thoughts to the ear of God (the creative force). The power of positive, intentional prayer to influence one's health and healing, among other things, has been proven in numerous scientific studies.

But what happens if our prayers are not positive? Here's an example of negative prayer by Joyce, whose husband is a police officer: "I worry about my husband when he's on-duty, so I stay tuned to the radio and television for news of robberies or gunfire involving officers." Joyce is waiting for something bad to happen, rather than focusing on seeing her husband safe. When Joyce dwells in negative prayers like that, she doesn't have to wait for bad news to happen in order to feel bad. By constantly worrying, she already feels awful.

Negative prayer limits your creator ability

Negative prayer includes:
* worrying
* complaining

> I was once asked why I don't participate in anti-war demonstrations.
>
> I said that I will never do that, but as soon as you have a pro-peace rally, I'll be there.
>
> ~ Mother Teresa

* perpetuating gossip
* obsessing, comparing, envying
* using statements such as "I can't"
* expecting bad things to happen.

If on a particular occasion you're finding it difficult to let go of worry, for instance, try this: Start by rounding up a few of the things that worry-mind is saying, write them out, and then write out what you *wish* would happen. From there, tell the truth about what you love unconditionally.

It might look something like this: Say you are having trouble writing a report for work. Every word is like pulling teeth. You're hating the work. How do you apply SWYL in this instance? Try saying this: "I love writing with ease and grace." Or, "I love loving my work." *For me, these are unconditionally true.* Or this: "I love completing projects." Find one or two statements that are true for you, that don't raise arguments. Then notice the truth of them, often. They don't cost a dime to notice, and you feel more powerful inside when you acknowledge the things you love.

Consider retiring your negative prayers. This is a huge step toward experiencing yourself as a creator being. Fill the available space with What You Love and watch your negative prayers shrivel up and drop away for lack of use.

To fret and worry is to pray for what you do not want to happen

Your word is your wand
Watch where you point that thing!

A mind is a terrible thing to waste. And the power of mind is wasted whenever you focus on what you want to avoid.

Consider how a computer works. It is a mass of circuits, wires and other components in a box. By itself, it merely sits there. It can't write a book or balance your checkbook until you tell it what to do. It's wired to follow your instructions precisely. For instance, if you are working on a spreadsheet, your computer won't suddenly begin spell checking your last letter— unless you tell it to.

Your mind works the same way. It does what you tell it to do. It can't think of ways to mend your marriage or improve your work situation if you have it wired to answer the question, "What's wrong with me that my wife loses interest?" That puts your mind to work on an entirely different task than when you declare, "I love being interesting to my wife!" This statement directs your attention to finding common ground and interests with her. It opens your mind so you notice your wife again and listen to her, instead of focusing on your own "why me" problems.

Your wife loses interest in you because you stop being interested in her. The outcome you're experiencing has its roots in what you ask your mind to pay attention to.

So if you are not getting the experiences or results you say you want, go back to your asking, and be clearer in where you point your attention. In other words, *point your wand*, direct your mind to the outcome you desire: "I love being attractive to my wife." Notice *where* this statement directs your attention: It's about *you*, not your wife. You access more power for creating What You Love when you communicate about you rather than about what you want other people to do. If you were to say "I want my wife to give me attention," you would be focusing on getting her to do something. That's anti-creating, and not as powerful as Saying What You Love.

Notice that this statement is about you in how it directs *your* attention. You have more power to create what you love when you communicate about you rather than what you need other people to do, for instance, "I love my wife giving me attention," which is about getting her to do something for you.

Access the right wand for the job!

Sometimes the best way to open to more joy may not be to ask for anything, but simply to Say What You Love.

Go straight to what you love!

When you forget to be in touch with what you love, it's usually because you are focused on the challenge in front of you and how to get rid of it. The world gives big points for attacking a problem aggressively. You hear advice like, "Get proactive." "You're a real go-getter" is considered a huge compliment. Yet attacking a problem in hopes of fixing it results in your working harder than is necessary. To attack, fix or struggle will limit your miracles. And when you forget to focus on What You Love, you settle for less.

Yes, tell the truth about what is happening. The car has broken down five miles from your kid's school. Then, go straight to What You Love. Don't bother with the middleman—you know, thoughts like, "Did I renew my Triple A? Who would come get me at this hour? I don't have more than ten bucks on me. My mechanic is way across town." For now, skip the middleman's concerns and questions, no matter how practical or justified they seem.

Instead, set a positive tone. Establish your vision by Saying What You Love. And, yes, you can do this even when your car has broken down. For example:

"I love feeling safe."

"I love being helped by wonderful people."

"I love having a phone to call the school so the teacher knows to have the kids wait a few minutes."

"I love being safely on the side of the road."

"I love having the car run well."

"I wonder what wonderful gift will come out of this little breakdown?"

Then, follow any intuitive hunches you have without analyzing them too much. By the way, those hunches may include some of the middleman's questions. The difference is you don't have to answer the whole barrage—only the ones that support your vision of What You Love.

Say What You Love. Watch what happens.

Chapter Six

Solve Problems
or
Create Miracles:

It's Your Choice!

Don't worry about the world
coming to an end today. It's
already tomorrow in Australia.

~Charles M. Schultz

Train your mind

Enlist your mind to work for your heart.

Remember, you get to choose. So give your mind a job
that moves you toward What You Love.

When you hear a thought that is anything other than
peaceful, get in the habit of asking, "What do I love?"

No matter what you're going through, ask:
Hmmmm. What do I love?

In the moment that you ask the question, "What do I love?"
you have enormous power. You are rewiring your brain to think
as a *Creator Being* instead of as a victim. Every opportunity you
take to ask that question is invaluable practice. You give yourself
the opportunity to choose. You can follow chaos, confusion or
emotional pain right down the drain, or you can take a breath and
tap into your native intelligence by noticing What You Love.

Sometimes, by mistake, all we do is trade one negative
thought for a less negative or nicer kind of thought. For example,
when "I hate rainy days on the weekend" is changed to "Ah, a lit-

tle rain can't ruin too much." That's okay, but not nearly as powerful as Saying What You Love. A direct way to heal that place deep inside the mind where negativity breeds is to focus on life-promoting love and light!

Now is always a good time to go within and find What You Love. Put your attention on what you love and watch negativity disappear due to lack of attention. Bravo!

Imagine a pitch dark room. No amount of effort trying to push out the dark will cause the room to be light. But if you open the blinds to the sun, voila! The light comes in. The dark disappears without further effort. *Where did the dark go?* To focus on a problem has about the same success rate as trying to push out the dark. Hopeless. Instead, put your attention on the light. Say What You Love. You'll see better.

Hear only love

See only love

Speak only love

TWO WOLVES
~author unknown

A Native American grandfather was talking to his grandson about how he felt about a recent tragedy.

He said, "I feel as though I have two wolves fighting in my heart. One wolf is the vengeful angry violent one. The other wolf is the loving, compassionate one."

The grandson asked, "Which wolf will win the fight in your heart?"

The grandfather answered, "The one I feed."

The allure of solving problems

When you've spent half your political life dealing with humdrum issues like the environment… it's exciting to have a *real crisis* on your hands.

~Margaret Thatcher, on the Falkland's Conflict

The habit of mental chaos, worry and focusing on problems is so alluring and seductive. It's automatic. It makes us feel important to do something. Anything! We feel valuable. The adrenaline flows. We are so mesmerized by crisis that we lose sight of what we love—yet love is the core and juice of our power.

The thing about succumbing to that allure is that you feed the issue, not the solution. The more you feed the problem, the more chaos, worry and dilemmas you'll have. Remember, you get what you pay attention to. *Is this making sense yet?* It will.

Try this:
If you were not obsessing over your
favorite problem right now, what would you
be feeling, doing or creating instead?

You know the issue—the problem that is like a broken record in your machine mind. The one that wakes you at four in the morning in full terrorizing technicolor. It's the one that always hooks you, that keeps you awake at night. It tricks you into thinking that you're not okay or not doing something right. It gives you lists of things you could or should do to or screams at you to run away. What's your favorite problem? Maybe it's: How do I keep from losing my youth (or my job, my home or my lover)? How do I stop my boss from firing me? How do I to get so-and-so to appreciate me? What's wrong with me that I can't manage to get into the college I want (earn good money, get pregnant, or travel wherever I want)?

A fascinating thing happens when you become aware of the underlying "What's wrong with me?" questions that play over and over again in the background of your mind. (The lists are endless.) You begin to see that the majority of your problems are like FEAR (False Evidence Appearing Real)— distractions, illusions.

When we fight one another, or worry about being attacked, we don't generate the creation energy that changes things. Fighting and worrying are distractions that trick people into thinking they are doing something important when all that's happening is a preoccupation with anti-creating.

Do you realize the prosperity that is available to every being on this planet if we would only begin to envision and live what we love rather keep anti-creating? You stop your flow of abundance when you *believe* in or try to *fix* poverty. There *is* enough for everyone. Put your attention on abundance, not lack of it. Then notice all the ways to access and share all the abundance.

"It looks like we'll be in position for war on Iraq by February if the diplomatic efforts don't complicate things."

~an American talk show host
December 2002
It's bizarre how this commentator would see a peaceful resolution as a complication to war.

If you have enough time to worry, you have time to Say What You Love

I love that no matter how bleak it looks, in one instant the blinds can open up to give way to light that guides the way.

For someone who spends their entire day occupied with basic survival—food, shelter, hygiene—Say What You Love may appear as a luxury that's available only for those who can afford the time. If you're spending 18 hours a day working, shuttling kids, doing laundry, making meals, cleaning house, and more, you might be thinking, "Who's got time to talk about love? Hey, nice little concept, but there is real work to be done. In fact, we need a third job just so the lights don't get turned off again this month." *Right?*

When you feel overwhelmed by day-to-day struggles, it can seem impossible to do anything more than put one foot in front of the other, nose glued firmly to the grindstone. "All I can do is get by the best I can," you might think. However, it is this *can't-do-any-better-than-this* attitude that keeps you stuck in the rut, digging yourself deeper and deeper into worry-mode—until you reach the point where you can't even remember what you love.

When you think about it, it's a sad way to pass through a life. Yet this is how many individuals, maybe most of us, spend much of our days.

It turns out this isn't just a personal issue. It has implications for society too. When so many individuals are stuck running in their own personal rat races, there are those with political or economic power who are happy to take advantage of your distraction. Before you know it, when you're busy worrying about the problems of your life, more restrictive laws, bureaucratic complexities and other infringements on your personal freedoms are slipped into place. Or the country goes about amassing troops in a buildup toward war that the people never sanctioned. Don't doubt for a minute that those in power aren't aware that when people are distracted by the struggle to survive, they rarely have the time or energy to question such questionable developments.

Yet, especially during the worst of times, there can be the greatest of transformations when we Say What We Love—right now. With so many beings paying attention to love, less attention is given to fear. Fear shrivels up when starved of attention. If the powers that be can't hook you into fear, you are free. You are free to be happy, and to help other people unhook from fear by modeling living peacefully What You Love, and sharing with others the value of saying What They Love.

This is a time of great spiritual growth in which great numbers of beings are awakening and becoming conscious. People in touch with their creator power will build a new world for themselves and others through their Say What They Love thoughts, visions and creations.

Naysayers may claim that one person saying what they love cannot change very much. But one being can create big movement and transformation. It happens all the time. If one stalled car on the freeway can back up hundreds of others in a matter of minutes, if one apple seed can make thousands of apples, surely one person can make a difference. You may surprise yourself and be that one person. Oh, and you are!

That's Mahatma Gandhi's story. He was an upper class lawyer until the day he was called to service by his own soul. Gandhi did not liberate India from the British by himself—but he did his part, by listening to and following his heart and speaking up about love and what was fair for the people. Gandhi discovered his own humanity through the process and stuck to his principles. In doing so, he inspired thousands of individuals to listen to their hearts and play their part in the peaceful liberation of India.

In the endearing movie I AM SAM, Sean Penn plays an adult man limited to a seven-year-old's mental functioning. Sam is an example of one person making a huge difference. He loves people consistently and patiently, and he tells the truth. One way he makes a difference to dozens of strangers a day is his way of talking to customers at the coffee shop where he works. "Tall double mocha skim latte' decaf. That's a wonderful choice, Bruce," he would say, addressing each customer by name and affirming their coffee selection.

Every time Sam says a customer's name, repeats their order and tells them that theirs is a wonderful choice, it feels so loving—like he is really saying, "You're smart; you matter; you are loved; have a wonderful day." I *lovvve* that! And it's free!!

Sam did not have to be a wealthy king before sharing his abundance, yet he made everyone around him feel rich and worthy.

Consider this: A CEO decides one day to make a difference. She takes half of her outrageous salary and stock options and redirects that money into the paychecks of 500 of the company's hourly workers. That could double the paychecks of nearly 500 workers or give a fifty percent increase to 1,000 employees a year. The CEO would still leave herself enough to enjoy a wonderful home, a summer cottage, a fabulous lifestyle, and an abundant retirement.

The salary increases for the employees would not only make a tremendous difference financially and morally to the 500 or 1,000 workers and their families. It would also inject millions of dollars into local communities, benefiting everyone who lives there.

Think about it. One CEO could change the lives of tens of thousands of people by doing that one thing. One being can do all that!

Each of us are in a unique position to make a difference even if we don't realize we are effecting a significant change. When you Say What You Love instead of adding negativity to a situation, there is no telling who you might influence or inspire.

To create or not create, that is the question

In any given moment, you are either creating or anti-creating. You create with each breath you take. Will it be a full life-giving breath or a shallow fear-based breath? You create with each word you speak or don't speak—"I can or can't do such-and-such"—and with every thought you think. You are so powerful that you even create the means to anti-create.

Create: to cause something unique to come into being or to evolve from one's imagination—a work of art or an invention. To create is to arrange or bring about, by intention or by choosing to create possibility in your life.

Anti–Create: a misconception about creating. If you have been working long and hard to achieve something, with little or no result, and no fun, you are anti-creating. To anti-create is to use faulty, limited or negative thinking strategies or behavior in an effort to avoid unpleasantness. For example, the statement "I didn't want to hurt your feelings," focuses on what you *don't* want and on the opposite of What You Love.

There is no try.
There is only do or not do.
~Yoda,
The Empire Strikes Back

Clues that you are Anti-creating:

You are anti-creating when you do any of the
following in an attempt to manifest something:

- ☒ Focus on problems, chaos or confusion, instead of what you love unconditionally.

- ☒ Justify. Argue. Second guess.

- ☒ Blame, shame, or lay guilt trips and "should" yourself.

- ☒ Try to figure out how to manifest something.

- ☒ Focus on avoiding an unpleasant or negative outcome. For example: "I don't want to get evicted," or "I don't want you to be mad at me."

- ☒ Give someone the silent treatment.

- ☒ Act passive-aggressive.

- ☒ Defend, over-guard, self protect, make threats.

- ☒ Obsess, worry, control. Give ultimatums.

You are anti-creating when you say things like:

- ☒ If I don't lay down the law, I won't get what I want.

- ☒ It's hopeless. It'll never happen. I'll never be able to …

- ☒ I want _____. I need _____. I wish _____. If only _____.

- ☒ I can't. I'll try.

- ☒ What's wrong with me? Why me?

- ☒ Nothing good ever happens to me.

- ☒ How will I get what I want if I don't point out what I don't like or want? If you loved me, you'd want to know. If you loved me, you'd know what I need.

- ☒ I don't need anything that fancy. Don't fuss.

- ☒ You better _____. You never _____. You always _____.

- ☒ How come bad stuff always happens to me?

- ☒ Why does she have all the luck?

- ☒ I don't care. Whatever.

- ☒ It never works out.

- ☒ Anything as simple as SWYL never works for me.

The optimist sees opportunity
in every danger;
the pessimist sees danger
in every opportunity.

~Winston Churchill

Creation Mode
~a simpler plan~

No matter what is happening around you,
or to you, or within you,
Say What You Love.

Acknowledge the "facts" and any temptation to indulge worry.
Then, choose to acknowledge and Say What You Love.

Even if it seems illogical or unattainable,
Say What You Love.

No matter if you think they'll laugh at you,
Say What You Love.

Don't be attached to the outcome or how you'll get it,
Say What You Love.

If you are confused, worried, scared or overwhelmed,
Say What You Love.

Even if you aren't confident in SWYL as a concept,
If it feels good, Say What You Love.

Chapter Seven

Power of Love

Generally, by the time you are
real, most of your hair has been
loved off, and your eyes drop out
and you get loose in the joints and
very shabby. But these things don't
matter at all, because once you
are **real**, you can't be ugly, except
to people who don't understand.

~Margery Williams
The Velveteen Rabbit

Practices for mastery

Here are several ways to explore and practice SWYL:

I wonder what I love now?

Ask this question and listen for the answer. It's coming. You don't have to make it up. This is not a test that you pass or fail. The answer comes because your brain is hot-wired to answer your questions.

This is a wonderful question, especially if you're just beginning to SWYL. Replace all your negative and anti-creation questions (such as "Why do I always screw things up?") with *this* one, "I wonder what I love now?" Ask it dozens of times throughout the day.

When you're in the rhythm of asking and listening for the answers to this question, you blaze new pathways for your brain to think lovingly and peacefully. You suddenly appear more brilliant because you are looking beyond the box of common limitations and suffering. So ask, "I wonder what I love? *Hmmm.*"

Be a Reporter of What You Love

Go through your day noticing What You Love. There will be no effort in this because you just *know*. You *know* What You Love like you *know* when you're hungry. You get a feeling. It's there. You have the power to ignore it for a little while, but the hunger is still there; eventually, hunger pangs are all you can think about if you let them go on too long.

If you *do* struggle to know What You Love, it probably means you're trying to figure out what other people think you should love, or what *you* think you should love.

Try this: *Be a reporter* to yourself of What You Love, without making up excuses, justifications, arguments, reservations or running an internal commentary of good or bad. (Remember, moral and loving behavior is built right into the SWYL concept.)

For instance, notice whatever you love about experiencing food and dining. It might be:

- ❤ I love eating right after a hot shower.
- ❤ I love warm soup on cold, windy days.

❤ I love doing the dinner dishes the next morning.

❤ I love walking around a farmers market — the smells, the music, the colors, the taste tests — and buying all my fresh food from the growers.

There is no good reason to give equal time to what you don't like or love. For example: "I loved the dinner; the meat loaf was just like grandma's. But I hated the lima beans." Or, "Wow, that is a really handsome man, but *why* does he dress like that?"

To create gold, just Say What You Love and leave off the negative commentary. Better yet, find What You Love even in your judgment. For instance, "I love when people are so confident they can dress that casually." Or, "I love how much joy it brings him to wear the shirt his grandma gave him." Or, "I love that I can see beauty no matter what."

If I say, "Imagine a green elephant in a bikini by a pool," there it is. Your imagination lets the picture come right up. It's the same with knowing what you love. All you have to do is *ask,* "What Do I Love?" and the answer comes to you. Use the following list to practice SWYL unconditionally without argument.

Report what you Love about:

breakfast
music
driving in rain
playing games
color
water
holidays
Sunday mornings
walking
fresh sheets
having a responsibility
the clothes you wear
danger
cooking
the beach
a summer day
bacon frying
asking a question
hearing a radio program
waiting
going to the dentist
someone saying "no" to you
The Super Bowl
window shopping

language
giving a gift
hugging
being still
being in motion
petting a cat
talking to a friend
mirrors
finishing a project
buying something new
getting caught in a fib
night time
your living space
bedtime stories
being in a body
being a man
being a woman
the person you are looking at
drinking water
traveling
rising to a challenge
loving someone & being loved
a kid's point of view
your parents

surprising someone
the wind
smiling
popcorn
flirting
an emotional movie
growing older
listening
sleeping in
throwing a dinner party
reading
Saying What You Love
snow
giggling
sealing an envelope
knowing Your Peace Counts
playing hooky from work
losing your cool
how you look
swimming
hearing chimes
Santa Claus
staying home sick
learning something new

Are you already making your own list? Great!

Pretend that no one can hear you unless you Say What You Love

"Your mouth is moving but I can't hear what you're saying."

What if this is how people responded to you all day? You walk into a meeting to present your carefully crafted plan, but everyone just looks at you blankly, their eyebrows squished together in confusion. They *sorta* see you, but can't hear you. All they can sense is noise, or a language they don't recognize.

But when you start Saying What You Love, all of a sudden they perk up in their chairs, obviously able to hear your plan.

How would your life be different if all the people in your life—colleagues, family, friends, acquaintances—could not hear your negativity, and they acted as if you were not even in the room.

How would your life be different if you received this kind of immediate feedback whenever you used anti-creation strategies? When you anti-create, you *do* actually get immediate feedback. It might not

We don't see things as they are,

we see them as we are.

~Anais Nin

take the form of people not seeing or hearing you. It usually just looks like arguing, defensiveness, walking on egg shells, resistance, "not getting what you want," or war.

We assume getting responses like these are normal just because they are common. What's truer is that this is the feedback we get whenever we are negative and not living what we love.

As an exercise, for a day (or an afternoon, an hour, a lunch date, or simply one conversation at a time), act *as if* people can only understand you when you speak from What You Love.

Catch yourself if you stray from Saying WYL. Restate yourself as many times as necessary. You can explain to those around you what you are training yourself to do, or not. If you notice that you would love to share your process with this person then do that. But don't do it because you think you *should*.

Life is so rich when you share from What You Love. *You inspire us all when you do,* especially if you chuckle at yourself whenever you find a new place where you forgot to speak from What You Love.

So, yes, please inspire us!

Making Room for Love

Would you love to see how big this love thing can get? Just how free would you love to be? The following exercise will clear you for take off. Clearing clutter opens blocked channels of pure energy.

Go to your closet and pull out 5 pieces of clothes, shoes or accessories that you haven't worn in 3 years.

Pick out 5 more things that are in disrepair (worn, torn or missing zippers, buttons, snaps) or that simply don't fit you anymore.

Then pick out 5 more things that you just don't love.

Put the 15 items in a bag to give to your local charity, or put them in the garbage if they are really tired. Get rid of this bag by the next day!

Repeat this process every week until you can't find anything else to put in the bag.

Then do this with every other room in the house— bed, bath and family rooms, kitchen, office (including computer files), attic, cupboards, shelves, counters, drawers, etc

Now, it's onto the porches, garage, yard, cars, your vacation cottage and storage lockers. *Oh, it feels so good!*

Empty Your Cup
~a story from Osho~

A monk went to the Zen Master to ask about God, nirvana, meditation, and so many things. The Master listened silently to all the questions and then he said, "You look tired. You have climbed this high mountain. Let me first serve you tea."

The monk was boiling with questions. He started thinking, "This whole journey is a waste. This old man is not wise. How can my question about God be answered by a cup of tea?"

continued ↗

. . . continued

The Master poured tea in the cup and went on pouring. Just one drop more and the tea would start flowing on the floor. The monk shouted, "Stop! What are you doing? Are you mad? Can't you see the cup and saucer are full?"

And the Zen Master said, "That's the exact situation you are in. Your mind is so full of questions, expectations and clutter, that you don't have space for new knowledge to go in.

"Since you entered this house your questions are overflowing all over the place.

"First empty your cup. Create a little space in yourself."

Use common sense of course.

Keep things like legal documents and family photos, even if you haven't looked at them in three years. But if you're done having children, get rid of those bags of maternity and baby clothes. Let someone else use them before the styles go out of fashion.

What about family heirlooms and keepsakes?

If you love them, go ahead and keep them. But there may be items in your house you think you *should* keep because they belonged to someone special. Those loved ones will remain special whether or not you keep their things. Release the burden you carry and discard any thing that doesn't fill you with comfort, happiness or big love, when you look at it. *Let their stuff go. It's okay.*

You'll probably discover that the emotional clutter tied up with that keepsake fades away when you get rid of the thing. And you'll create more room to remember your special people fondly, without guilt, if you keep only the stuff of theirs that you love. Make room for *big love* to surround you and live within you.

You make room for more love in your heart and in your life when you clean out the clutter—the clutter in your head, in your home and in your body.

There are many kinds of clutter

Mental clutter is that negative thinking that drones on and on in your head. Saying What You Love addresses that kind of clutter beautifully.

Home clutter is the piles of magazines you're going to read someday, the stacks of who-knows-what, closets filled to the brim, garages full of unfinished projects and fix-it-someday-jobs.

This clutter blocks the flow of vital energy and abundance. This is why you want to go room by room and declutter the old, the broken, and the not loved. Through this process, you keep what you love, release what you don't, and reveal a nurturing and revitalizing home full of everything you *lovvve*.

Clutter in the body is the toxic build-up left behind from food that does not combine well, or digest well, or that gives anti-bio yeasts and parasites a chance to thrive. Toxic build-up affects your clarity, vitality, emotions, and experience of love and peace. It's simply trickier to live what you love when your body is muddied by inner pollutants.

Cellulite and pudgy spots are less about over-eating than about a toxic overload that compromises your body's digestion of fats. Instead of attacking fat or counting calories, put your atten-

~WHY~
oh why, would you
want to keep a thing
that you don't love
and which doesn't
bring you joy or comfort
to look at or use?

> Going to a church doesn't make you a Christian any more than going to a garage makes you an automobile.
>
> ~Billy Sunday

tion on detoxifying your colon, liver and other organs in an educated, enthusiastic and dedicated way.

It's true that both toxins and fat are clutter, but paying attention to releasing toxins is a more efficient way to declutter than worrying about calories and fat.

It's the difference between taking out the garbage regularly (de-toxifying) or complaining that garbage bags are piling up to the ceiling in your kitchen and wondering which diet to go on next to make the bags smaller.

Cleanse your body regularly by drinking half your body weight in ounces of pure water daily, and through a diet of fresh alkaline foods, elimination of parasites and bio-antagonistic yeasts, and with loving wholistic colonics.

One welcome resource for regenerating your body is Donna Gate's book *The Body Ecology Diet*.

Go have fun learning how to love your body by keeping it clean and uncluttered. Saying What You Love about feeling healthy and looking great may make your detoxifying mission easier. And being less cluttered in your body makes it easier for you to Say What You Love. You can only win.

Ask others to Say What They Love

Be sure to ask others to report on What They Love. You really get to know someone this way. And you can jumpstart a relationship or a conversation with SWYL.

Asking someone What They Love is a refreshing way to uplift a negative interaction. It's an especially effective tool in situations that are confusing or argumentative.

Instead of the usual "What did you do today?" try asking, "What did you love today?" or "What did you love about what you did today?"

At parties, instead of the familiar "What do you do?" you might ask, "What do you love about what you do?" or "When was the last time you thought about what you love unconditionally?"

How would you be different if:

How would your life be different today if whenever you described something or asked for something you said what you loved?

How would your meal times be different if all your topics gravitated toward what you each love?

How would your meal selections be different if you chose food based on what you love *unconditionally* —which means without argument, justification or dread of heartburn, indigestion or weight gain?

How would your relationships be different if you each were asking, giving and reporting based on what you each love *unconditionally*?

How much more brilliant and expressive would your children be, and your teaching and caring for them be, if you focused on what you love about them? (Even when you're correcting their behaviors, remember to notice What You Love.)

How different would you be today if you performed your obligations in the spirit of SWYL?

I have found the best way to give advice to your children is to find out what they love and then advise them to do it.

~Harry S. Truman

The Power of Meditation

Take time to be still. It's a tall order in a fast world, but if you choose to do it, the dividends will be huge and can't be matched. When you're quiet and listen, you hear your heart's wisdom.

Being in nature helps with deep stillness. And you can create a sacred space for meditation wherever you are. At home, this could be a whole room dedicated to meditation or a little corner of any room. Have your place to sit, a cozy blanket for chilly mornings, quiet music, inspirational reading, pictures or statues of inspiring beings, incense—whatever encourages you to keep this appointment with your beingness. Come and *be* here, with no agenda but to relax, be still, and reconnect to *Self*.

Out in the marketplace, try using a pair of earplugs to help with quiet in noisy restaurants, airports, and other public places. It is truly amazing how valuable a little muffling can be.

And do take advantage of those precious moments before you drift off to sleep and when you first awaken. Silently connect with your being, breathing fully. Reflect on the day gone by or ahead of you. Notice What You Love about your day and the people you interacted with. Recognize your freedom to express your love in the day ahead. Bless your days as they come and go.

*Silence is
the language God speaks.
Everything else
is a poor translation.*

~Eckhart Tolle

The Power of loving Self

In a quiet moment, ask yourself if you love having or doing any of the following experiences outlined below. If some of these things seemed like an effort before, perhaps you tried to do them out of obligation to, domination over, or denial of your body. Those strategies are anti-creating and they don't inspire joy in caring for your sweet Self. Noticing What You Love about self-care clears a pathway and creates a rhythm that eases the way. Now, ask yourself if you love each of the following.

❤ I love being hydrated. I love the freedom of movement I get from being hydrated. I love my joints being happy. I love my bowels moving effortlessly. I love thinking clearly. And I *lovvve* having lots of energy.

❤ I love eating foods that make me feel better. I love my stomach being happy and my digestion working like clockwork. I love having more energy after I eat. I love eating foods that make me sleep and dream well.

❤ I love feeling every muscle being alive and happy. I love stretching 15-30 minutes each day—back, legs,

❤ arms, neck, joints, sides, hands, feet, and the con-
nective tissue in between. A yoga session, Tibetan
Five Rites (*Fountain of Youth*), martial arts, Arica,
imitating the nearest stretching cat — it's all good.

❤ I love fresh air. I love being outside breathing fresh
air. I love the way my hair and clothes smell after
being in fresh air. I love the aliveness in my lungs
breathing real air out of doors.

❤ I love being rested. I love getting all the sleep my
body needs and the yummy feeling that gives me
when I wake up. I love sleeping long enough to have
those deep, amazing dreams.

❤ I love feeling connected to my friends and loved
ones. I love walking in nature with a friend or two. I
love loving them. I love hearing their voices. I love
hearing what they love. I love giving and receiving
fun little care packages when we're apart. I love
email and notes and cards and phone calls with my
loved ones.

❤ I love laughter. I love sincerity. I love watching
whales at sunset. I love walking under a full moon.

"I hear what you don't want. Now, tell yourself what you love."

Anti–Creation Statements	THE GRAY AREA. Are you: anti-creating or taking a step toward SWYL?	Say What You Love is pure creation
I don't want to lose the game. I hate to lose.	I'll try to not lose. I want to win the game.	I love to play to win. I love to win at what I love.
I don't want them to see me fail.	I want to look good to them.	I love succeeding at whatever I love to do.
I don't want to go home a loser.	I want to go home a winner.	I love to go home and share what I love about my day.
I don't want to get in trouble.	I want to not be fired. I want to keep my job.	I love expressing myself freely at work, and I love being authentic in my work.
I hate you being mad at me.	Don't be mad at me. I don't want to make you mad.	I love being a safe space for loved ones. I love being easy to love. I love honest emotion.
I'll try not to do anything wrong.	I'll try to do it right.	I love expressing my joy. I love expressing what works.

SAY WHAT YOU LOVE Unconditionally

Anti-Creation Statements	THE GRAY AREA. Are you: anti-creating or taking a step toward SWYL?	Say What You Love is pure creation
I want there to be no war.	I want them to stop war. I want peace.	I love peace. I love being peaceful. I love contributing to peace.
I don't want to be so stubborn.	I want people to not push me. I want to be more flexible.	I love flowing with the rhythm. I love being flexible.
I'm so tired of not getting what I want.	When is it my turn to get what I want? I want what I want.	I love feeling supported. I love _____.
I want to stop comparing myself.	I want to be comfortable being myself.	I love celebrating who I am and what I'm up to.
I need a new job.	I want a great new job.	I love getting paid for what I love to do.
I wish people cared about each other and would get along.	I want people to be nice to one another and get along.	I love caring about people. I love _____.
I want to have enough money to travel wherever I want.	I want to travel wherever I want.	I love traveling wherever I love. I love _____.

Power of Love

166

Play around today with not using words like *want, don't want, need, don't need, can't,* and *I'll try.*

Don't think of these as words you can't or shouldn't use. Just notice when you've used them, and think of them as red flags. These flags signal you to fine-tune your creative powers and point you in the direction of pure creation.

The joy and power of Say What You Love is so simple that it is within your capability to master with only a little practice. Do your own research to confirm this for yourself. Begin by simply replacing your anti-creation language with saying what you love. If doing this instills a sense of ease or peace within you, or brings a smile to your face, perhaps you'll try it again tomorrow. Don't be surprised if Saying What You Love grows on you and starts being easy to do—as if you're being guided from within. You are. *Your love is guiding you now.*

~Imagine~

Imagine all the people

living life in peace.

You may say I'm a dreamer;

but I'm not the only one.

I hope someday you'll join us,

and the world will be as one.

~John Lennon

Glossary of Creation and Anti-Creation Words

The limits of my language
are the limits of my world.

~Ludwig Wittgenstein

GLOSSARY of Creation and Anti-Creation Words

Defining the territory between creating or blocking what you love.

The following definitions are drawn from widely used dictionaries, except as indicated by brackets [ ]. Consult your dictionary for common words not found in this glossary.

ability *n.* 1) power or capacity to do or act physically, mentally, legally, morally, or financially. 2) aptitude based on natural or acquired capacity to do things.

acknowledge *v.t.* 1) to admit to be real or true. 2) recognize the existence, truth, or fact of.

affirmation *n.* the assertion that something exists or is true.

anti-Create *v.* [1) to block or hinder creation. 2) the act of using faulty, limited or negative thinking or behavior, such as worry. 3) seeking to produce a desired result by trying to avoid unpleasantness. 4) to focus on the opposite of what is true. 5) to focus on the opposite of what one loves.]

argument *n.* 1) a statement, reason, or fact for or against a point.

ask *v.* 1) inquire of. 2) to request: *to ask a favor.* 3) to demand; expect. 4) to call for; need. 5) to invite. 6) to make inquiry. 7) to request or petition.

authentic *adj.* 1) genuine, real, reliable, trustworthy. 2) having an origin supported by unquestionable evidence. 3) originating in native, unquestionable truth. [root word: *author*— the maker of anything; creator; originator.]

authority *n.* 1) an expert on a subject [*You are the authority on your own heart and inner.*] 2) the right to control, command, or determine [one's vision and actions.] 3) the power to determine, or otherwise settle issues [as in conflicts between heart and mind; and between internal authority vs. external authorities.]

be *v.* [an action] 1) to exist or live: *Shakespeare's "To be or not to be" is the age old question.* 2) to take place; occur: [*He had a way of being friendly*]. 3) to occupy a place or position. *[a way of being]*

being *n.* *[a being]* 1) a living thing. 2) a human being. 3) God. 4) something that exists.

beingness *n.* [authentic presence: *Gandhi's beingness inspired a nation.*]

bond *n.* [Black's Law Dictionary: 1) a bond is evidence of a debt. 2) a promise to do or pay something. 3) a promise to transfer energy.] [*My word is my bond.*]

breathe *v.* 1) to take air, oxygen, etc., into the lungs and expel it; inhale and exhale. 2) to live, exist. 3) to express; manifest. 4) **breathe freely,** to have relief from anxiety, tension, or pressure.

cause *n.* a person that acts or a thing that occurs so as to produce a specific result: *the cause of the damage.*

choice *n.* 1) an act or instance of choosing; selection. 2) the right, power, or opportunity to choose; option. 3) implies the ability and opportunity to choose freely.

create *v.* 1) to cause something you love to come into being. 2) to evolve from one's imagination, as a work of art or an invention.

creation *n.* 1) the act of creating. 2) the fact of being created. 3) something that is created. 4) the creation, the original bringing into existence of the universe by

SAY WHAT YOU LOVE *Unconditionally*

God.

creative *adj.* having the quality or power of creating.

creator *n.* 1) a person or thing that creates. 2) the creator, God. [*You*].

creator Being *n.* [1) one who acknowledges, accepts, and participates as a creative cause. 2) native intelligence and ability to envision into existence. 3) one who perceives, envisions, or behaves with creative power and intent.]

desire v. 1) to wish or long for; crave, want. 2) to ask for; solicit; request. 3) a longing or craving, as for something that brings satisfaction; hunger. 4) an expressed wish; request. 5) something desired.

empowered *v.t.* to endow with an ability; enable.

envision *v.t.* to picture mentally some future event [or experience].

exercise *n.,v.,* 1) bodily or mental exertion, especially for the sake of training or improvement. 2) forms of practice designed to train, develop, condition, etc. 3) put into action, use, or effect: the exercise of imagination.

fear *n.* 1) a distressing emotion aroused by impending danger, evil, pain, etc., whether the threat is real or imagined. 2) concern. [FEAR: false evidence appearing real.]

fearful adj. 1) feeling fear or anxiety. 2) causing or apt to cause fear: *fearful behavior.*

free *adj.* 1) able to act or think without compulsion or arbitrary restriction. 2) enjoying personal rights or liberty, as one who is not in slavery or confinement (whether mentally or physically).

free will *n.* the doctrine that the conduct of human beings expresses personal choice and is not simply determined by physical or divine forces.

grok v. 1) to understand thoroughly and intuitively. 2) to communicate harmoniously. {coined by Robert A. Heinlein in the sci-fi novel *Stranger in a Strange Land* (1961)}

illusion *n.* something that deceives by producing a false or misleading impression of reality.

imagination *n.* 1) the action or faculty of forming mental images or concepts of what is not actually present to the senses. 2) the product of imagining; a conception or mental creation. 3) ability to face and resolve difficulties; resourcefulness.

intuitive hunch *n. a* perception or a knowing about something. [a feeling or thought that you could act or follow up on: *I had an intuitive hunch that someone at the party would have a good answer for my dilemma.*]

isness *adj.* [native presence of love, peace, harmony. the reality of a situation or thing; *The Isness of love cannot be underestimated.*]

Justify *v.* 1) to show or prove to be just, right, or reasonable. 2) to defend. **—justification** *n.*

know *v.* 1) to perceive or understand as fact or truth. 2) to recognize: [*I know that in my bones*]. 3) to be acquainted or familiar with (a thing, place, person, feeling, etc.). 4) to be cognizant or aware.

love *n.,v.,* 1) a profoundly tender, passionate affection for another. 2) affectionate concern for the well-being of others. 3) a strong predilection, enthusiasm, or liking. 4) to have love or affection for. 5) to feel the emotion of love. 6) infused with or feeling deep affection or passion (for); enamored (of).

machine mind *n.* [1) a person or thing that acts in a mechanical or automatic manner. 2) automatic or habitual negative thinking; chaotic, defensive, or negative mental thoughts arising or repeating in the mind in a nonstop manner. 3) fearful or fear-based thinking as a reference point for making decisions.]

manifest *adj.* 1) readily perceived by the eye or the understanding. 2) visible. —*v.t.* to make clear or evident to the eye or the understanding: *to manifest [friendship].*

manifestation *n.* 1) an act of manifestation. 2) an outward or perceptible indication; materialization; a public demonstration.

manipulate *v.* 1) to manage or influence skillfully and often unfairly; to manipulate people's feelings. 2) to suit one's purpose or advantage.

mesmerize *v.t.* 1) to hypnotize. 2) spellbind; fascinate. 3) to compel by fascination.

mind-body *adj.* taking into account the physiological, psychic, and spiritual connections between the state of the body and that of the mind: *mind-body medicine.*

miracle *n.* 1) a superb or surpassing example of something wondrous; a marvel. 2) an extraordinary occurrence that surpasses all known human powers or natural forces and is ascribed to a divine or supernatural cause, especially to God.

native *adj.* 1) belonging to a person by birth or to a thing by nature; inherent: *native* ability. 2) *go native,* to imitate the behavior of a surrounding culture, esp. behavior that seems simple or natural.

need *n.* 1) a requirement, necessary duty, or obligation. 2) a lack of something wanted or deemed necessary. 3) urgent want. 4) a situation or time of difficulty. 5) a condition marked by the lack of something requisite. 6) destitution; extreme poverty.

peace *n.* 1) a state of harmony between people or groups. 2) freedom from anxiety, annoyance, or other mental disturbance: *peace of mind*. 3) a state of tranquility or serenity. 4) silence; stillness. 5) untroubled.

power *n.* 1) *ability* to do or act; capability of doing or accomplishing something. 2) a person or thing that possesses or *exercises* authority or influence. 3) energy, force, momentum. —*v.t.* 1) to supply with electricity or other means of power [such as your intention, juiciness and love.] 2) to give power to; make powerful. 3) to inspire. 4) to supply force to operate [a thought, vision or mission]. —*adj.* conducting electricity; a power cable [as in between your heart and mind]. —**Powers** *n.* a deity; divinity: *the heavenly powers.*

powerless *adj.* 1) unable to produce an effect; ineffective. 2) lacking power to act; helpless. [3) characterized by use of anti-creation methods.]

prayer *n.* 1) a devout petition to God or object of worship. 2) a spiritual communion with God. 3) something prayed for.

problem *n.* 1) any question or matter involving doubt, uncertainty, or difficulty.

reservation *n.* 1) the act of keeping back, withholding, or setting apart.

say *v.* 1) to utter or pronounce; speak: *to say the word.* to express in words (a message or viewpoint). 2) to speak; declare; express an opinion, idea, etc.

sovereign *n.* 1) rightful status, independence, or prerogative [of every human]. 2) the status, dominion, power, or authority of a sovereign.

story *n.* 1) a narrative, either true or fictitious. 2) a fictitious tale.

truth *n.* 1) the true or actual state of a matter. 2) the state or character of being true. 3) actuality or actual existence. 4) honesty; integrity; truthfulness. 5) ideal or fundamental reality apart from, and transcending, perceived experience.

unconditionally *adv.* 1) not limited by conditions; absolute. [*unconditionally aligned with and resulting in peace* without argument, reservation, or justification.]

vision *n.* 1) the power to anticipate a future or that which may come to be; foresight: *entrepreneurial vision.* 2) a vivid, imaginative anticipation.

want *v.t.* 1) to feel a need or a desire for; wish for: *to want a new dress.* 2) to be deficient in. 3) to be in a state of neediness or poverty. —*n.* 1) absence or deficiency; lack: *for want of rain.* 2) a state of destitution; poverty. —**Wanting** *adj.* 1) lacking or absent. 2) deficient in some part or respect.

well-being *n.* 1) a good or satisfactory condition of existence. 2) a state characterized by health, happiness, and prosperity.

what 1) used to inquire as to the origin of something. 2) used to inquire as to the worth, usefulness, force, or importance of something.

wish *v.t.* to want; desire; long for: *I wish to travel. I wish it were morning.* —*n.* 1) an expression of a kindly or courteous nature: *to send one's best wishes.* 2) something wished or desired: *to get one's wish.*

worry *v.* 1) to feel uneasy or anxious; torment oneself with or suffer from disturbing thoughts; fret. 2) to move with effort, anxiety, apprehension. 3) to disturb with annoyance; plague.

you *pron.* [Yes, *you*!]

The object of love is to serve,
not win.

~Woodrow Wilson

Visit us on the web at:

SayWhatYouLove.com

or

or YourPeaceCounts.com

We love to receive your stories by email.

How has Saying What You love Unconditionally
influenced your decisions, attitudes and sensibilities.

or

How has living What You Love Unconditionally changed your life—
your relationships, your work, your prosperity?

or

How has living Say What You Love Unconditionally changed your —
sense of joy, accomplishment, peacefulness?

Please share your copy of Say What You Love with loved ones.
Or gift a friend, or group a friends, each with their own.

Thank you!
Your Peace Counts Foundation